Technical Writing in Action

Technical Writing in Action

PRACTICAL APPLICATIONS FOR STEM STUDENTS

First Edition

Jon Negrelli
Cleveland State University

cognella®
SAN DIEGO

Bassim Hamadeh, CEO and Publisher
Jennifer Codner, Senior Field Acquisitions Editor
Michelle Piehl, Senior Project Editor
Christian Berk, Associate Production Editor
Jess Estrella, Senior Graphic Designer
Greg Isales, Licensing Associate
Natalie Piccotti, Director of Marketing
Kassie Graves, Vice President of Editorial
Jamie Giganti, Director of Academic Publishing

Cover image copyright © 2019 iStockphoto LP/metamorworks.

Printed in the United States of America.

cognella | ACADEMIC PUBLISHING

3970 Sorrento Valley Blvd., Ste. 500, San Diego, CA 92121

Contents

Preface

Technical Writing in Action

Practical Applications for STEM Students

This textbook is the result of a critical need for classroom activities in the Technical Communications and Professional Writing classroom. After surveying students for the last eight years, we find that not all students enjoy the lecture style of teaching. Many of them would like to reinforce their studies by working with their peers on lecture-related projects and activities. After compiling these activities over a period of several years, the result is a unique collection of exercises that could benefit students studying Science, Technology, Engineering, and Mathematics (STEM).

By working in small groups, students put into practical use the readings from the classroom lecture. The substance of the lecture is understood once students attempt to fulfill the requirements of the associated project.

There are many textbooks that teach grammar, punctuation, and sentence structure; this is not one of them. It is an opportunity for students to engage in activities they will encounter in their professional lives. After leaving school, students are expected to have a certain understanding of the documents and research in which they will participate. Some of these projects present a new perspective into everyday writing, and some of them will be infrequently used yet very important in the overall education of STEM students. This book not only presents students with the opportunity to create these documents, but also gives them an understanding of the underlying structures of good document creation from the viewpoint of the reader's expectations.

The book favors the process used in designing instructional material by incorporating the five steps of

- Analyzing
- Designing
- Developing

- Implementing
- Evaluating

Students are, in effect, creating their own instruction in the way they learn.

Other textbooks may include exercises at the end of each chapter, but they are rarely used. Students and instructors often view these as problematic as they include little explanation; they simply state a problem with little or no consideration for solving the issue.

The approach used in this textbook is geared to learning from others in a group setting. Everyone is involved and has a chance to contribute to solving a problem. In a lecture situation, some or all material is misunderstood or not deemed necessary by the student, who may neglect taking complete notes. In a group situation, the common knowledge shared by all becomes more significant as everyone has a chance to contribute. Students are more engaged and contribute more often when they are not afraid of being criticized in front of the whole class for being wrong.

It is permitted to make mistakes; students can sometimes learn more from their mistakes than their lectures.

NOTE: The lessons in this textbook require the use of software such as Microsoft Office© (any version after 2003) or the open source version titled Apache Open Office© available at http://www.openoffice.org/download/.

For Chapter 5 on graphics, there are products from Adobe available on a trial basis such as Photoshop© or Illustrator©.

Open source software such as GIMP (GNU Image Manipulation Program) works well with most images used online or for presentations. For a good open source program like Illustrator© try InkScape© available at https://inkscape.org/.

Introduction

Technical Writing in Action

Practical Applications for STEM Students

"Tell them what you're going to tell them,

Tell them,

Tell them what you just told them."[1]

High school students, college students, and graduates involved in the STEM fields can all benefit from the activities included in this textbook. It can be used for either obtaining new knowledge or reviewing universal technical writing forms. Plot, character development, and poetic devices covered in creative writing classes are of little concern. Technical communication differs from other styles of writing as the main goal of the writer is to achieve clarity.[2]

This book is a collection of activities and projects that can be used in collaboration with an instructor's lecture or as a stand-alone reference for writing technical documents. The lessons are focused on providing an outcome deemed necessary to achieve strong writing skills. It is one thing to read about document structure, research, and public presentation, but quite another to experience it as a complete activity.

Each chapter contains the information needed to complete the assignment by presenting these main sections:

---

1   Quote is attributed to Aristotle, *Rhetoric*, 350 BCE. Earliest print reference is Northern Daily Mail, "Three Parts of a Sermon," Durham, England, 1908.

2   A. Rand, *The Art of Nonfiction: A Guide for Writers and Readers* (London: Penguin Books, 2001), 2.

1. **Introduction.** This section states the purpose of the exercise so that the reader understands what is expected of them in solving the problem. It sets a clear path for the student to perform each of the steps with a successful outcome.

2. **Project Overview.** This section assists the reader in performing the initial research for the project. It can be considered an initial investigation or fact-finding mission.

3. **Project Design.** Every written document should follow a clear design that presents the reader with an underlying template written in a logical voice.

4. **Project Development.** Once the template is completed, it is time for placing the information into a recognizable format, one that the reader expects and that is written with clarity.

5. **Peer Review.** This is the evaluation section of the assignment. Before submitting the project for grading, the students discuss their findings and performance with others in the class. This is where the real learning takes place. By receiving input from their peers about the project, each participant learns from their mistakes and the mistakes of others.

The chapters in the book follow a logical sequence with certain lessons dependent on the knowledge learned in previous chapters. However, you may find that many of the projects work well on their own, by selecting them as needed.

It is imperative for STEM students to understand the importance of relating their research to others in a clear manner. This would ensure that anyone else striving to re-enact the findings of one person would be able to do so by following the findings of their research.

Once these projects have been completed, students realize that it is a simple matter to write a clear document. They can construct one using a conventional format, or create their own using three basic rules of writing:

1. *Introduction.* Tell them what you're going to tell them.
2. *Body.* Tell them.
3. *Conclusion.* Tell them what you just told them.

CHAPTER ONE

Writing a Professional Email

Estimated time to complete: 20–30 minutes

INTRODUCTION

Emails have become one of the most popular forms of communication for both business and personal use. In this activity you will review the basic parts of the email and understand the best use of each of these areas. After this, you will correct an actual email sent by a professional engineer to a graphic artist and eliminate the mistakes in the message that may cause confusion. This activity covers email etiquette, proper use of the email workspace, and an activity in correcting and rewriting a poorly written email.

PROJECT OVERVIEW

The information you will need to successfully complete this project is listed below in the form of a checklist. It is important to consider how the receiver of your message will understand each section of the email interface, what the receiver expects to see, and what you have sent them.

When Should You Send an Email?

Emails are a great way of communicating a formal request to someone from another company, institution, or organization. It is not as invasive as a phone call and yet will be considered important enough to be read by the receiver. If you wish your message to be viewed as worthwhile, follow these basic guidelines.

SIDE BOX 1.1:
Understanding the User Experience (UX)

The international standard on ergonomics of human system interaction, ISO 9241-210:
   According to the ISO definition, user experience includes all the users' emotions, beliefs, preferences, perceptions, physical and psychological responses, behaviors, and accomplishments that occur before, during, and after use. The ISO also lists three factors that influence user experience: system, user, and the context of use. [1]

   "... the quality of experience a person has when interacting with a specific design." [2]

---

[1]   International Organization for Standardization (2009). "Ergonomics of human system interaction—Part 210: Human-centered design for interactive systems (formerly known as 13407)." ISO F±DIS 9241-210:2009.

[2]   User Experience Network, "About UXnet," http://uxnet. org/, viewed July 23, 2018.

Checklist for Email Etiquette and Format

- **DO:** *Include a meaningful subject line.* Make sure that this is something that can sum up your message in just a few words. If this message needs to be reviewed in the future, the user will search for key words in the message and typically these are found in the *subject line.*
- **DO:** *Use a formal greeting.* If you are not on familiar terms with the receiver be sure to use a formal greeting.
- **DO:** *Use standard spelling, punctuation, and capitalization.* Your message will be more believable if you acknowledge this rule. Avoid using three-letter acronyms, slang, and other informal types of communication.
- **DO:** *Write clear, short paragraphs and be direct and to the point.* Brevity is important. Do not go off on a tangent talking about the latest kitty video on the internet.
- **DO:** When sending attachments, state the file name in the body of the message. If the file is downloaded and misplaced, this will give the user an easy way to search their computer for the file, provided that it has a unique, searchable name.
- **DO:** *When writing instructions, use bullet points.* This will make it easier for the user to distinguish the steps in a process they are to follow. If it is necessary to follow a specific order, use a numbered list.
- **DON'T:** *Joke around, be polite and courteous.* Fun and games may come later once you are on a personal level with the receiver.

- **DO:** *Include alternate contact information.* This would help if the person receiving your email finds it necessary to talk to you regarding some unclear items.
- **DON'T:** *Write something you will regret in the future.* Once you hit the "send" button your message cannot be retrieved.
- **DO:** *Use an appropriate closing statement.* Try to match the level of formality you have established in your greeting.

PROJECT DESIGN

Design the message as the reader expects it to look, often referred to as the *user experience* (UX). In the case of an email, the design is already done for you in a format that the receiver understands and expects.

There are options available to you to implement within the structure of the email program. For example, you could add your contact information to the bottom of the email window so that it always appears there. It would also save you time instead of rewriting it every time you send an email.

PROJECT DEVELOPMENT

The following is an actual email written by a professional engineer to a graphic artist. The message is very unclear because the engineer did not follow the basic guidelines for writing a formal email.

1. Mark the mistakes that distract you from the message this engineer is trying to convey.
2. Rewrite the message in clearer terms with the help of the checklist in today's project.

TABLE 1.1 *Email to correct*

To: carl123

From: engineer01

Subject: Some drawings

Hey Carl

How ya doin?

I'm still working on the new stuff, I will have a bunch for you in about a week maybe thursday. Mostly redoing animations to current standards. For figure 3-23 the multi stage generator pic the tubes are great but remove the "arrowheads", remove the numbers, make the first box RED and the bottom blue, show the blue streaking into to the red as it progresses across.

There should be definitele lines from the box on the bottom showing flow through the gates (See attached file: multi stage generator.jpg)

Ok?

me

<SUBMIT>

In the space below, rewrite the message so that it is easier to understand.

Be sure to correct grammar, spelling, and punctuation.

TABLE 1.2 *Your corrected version of the email*

To: carl123

From: engineer01

Subject:

<SUBMIT>

PEER REVIEW

Although you were able to correct the obvious errors in grammar, punctuation, and spelling, you probably discovered that it was difficult to decipher the meaning of some parts of the exercise. That is one of the difficulties you must overcome in your writing. Try to be clear in all your communications by understanding the reader's viewpoint. Clarity is everything.

Have someone else review the corrections you have made to this email, and you may also review another student's work. You will find that there are many alternate solutions to this problem.

Learn from the suggestions from your peers as well as from your mistakes. The things you will remember the most are the corrections to your mistakes.

VOCABULARY

decipher
ergonomics
etiquette
peer
user experience (UX)

CHAPTER TWO

Testing Your Resume

Estimated time to complete: 30–40 minutes

INTRODUCTION

You should have a simple resume completed by this time in your life. Although a great resume is important in landing your dream job, it is just a small part of the whole interview process. In this project, you will apply for a job to see how all the pieces fit together for a successful application. Three documents are needed to complete this exercise: your resume, a cover letter, and a printout of a job description.

PROJECT OVERVIEW

Go online to search for a job that would be your ideal type of employment. Once you have found a job that interests you, print out the description of that job, and most important, the job *requirements* (or qualifications). You will need this information to properly complete this project. It would be a benefit to you if you select an opportunity within your field of study.

Resume	Job Description	Cover Letter
Education _____	Must be able to _____	Yes, I am able to _____
Experience _____	_____	_____
References _____	_____	_____
	_____	

FIGURE 2.1   Three Part Exercise.

Update Your Resume

The way your future employer will determine if you are their ideal candidate is by matching your experience and education with the requirements for this job position. The more of these that you possess, the better your chances of landing an interview (the first step in the hiring process). Your resume contains the *information* about you and your achievements by outlining your education, work experience, contact information, and activities.

A good resume is constructed so that the reader may easily select the areas that relate to the job opening they wish to fulfill. Therefore, there should be recognizable sections with bold headings to separate the information on the page.

There are some things that should never be included in your resume. Very often this information is not necessary to qualify for the position, and may even be illegal for the interviewer to discuss with you.

Never include the following:

- Race
- Religion
- Marital status
- Age
- Disabilities

When looking at your resume, draw a vertical line and a horizontal line through the middle to divide it into four quadrants.

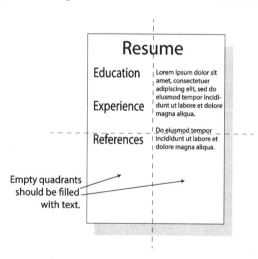

FIGURE 2.2   Quadrant Test.

Then make a visual test of your resume to be sure that there is an equal amount of text in each quadrant. This will give your document an appealing look.

Find Your Ideal Job Description

Begin your search for the ideal job by doing an online search at any of the major job sites. It could be a job you are seeking for temporary employment, a career position you are looking forward to, or a company that you wish to work for.

- Write the name of the job description:

  _____

- Write the contact information listed for this position. A contact name may be omitted from the listing. If this is the case, you may refer to the *Human Resources Department* or a similar name in your cover letter. Be sure to write the street address, city, state, and zip code.

  _____

  _____

  _____

- Every job description should have a section labeled *requirements* or *qualifications* for the advertised position. Find this section in the job description, and then list as many of these as you can find in the space below. These requirements are an essential part of this project.

  _____

  _____

  _____

SIDE BOX 2.1:
Using Text as a Placeholder

Very often publishers will use text in Latin as a placeholder. It usually begins with the words "Lorem ipsum ..." to let the reader know that there is new text coming to fill that space (see Figure 2.2).

Write a Formal Cover Letter to the Company or Organization

The cover letter will most likely be the first thing the employer will view in the hiring process. The cover letter contains the persuasive element you present to the employer to demonstrate your ability to perform this position. Be sure that it includes all the necessary formalities necessary to introduce yourself to someone who does not know you. Most important, in this letter you will prove to the reader that you meet the requirements posted in the job description.

PROJECT DESIGN

Design the message as the reader expects it to look. Many templates are available to you for the resume and for the formal cover letter. Select the one that best reflects and complements your personal taste. If you are using paper with a preformatted header, such as a logo, be sure to adapt the whole printout to consider this.

PROJECT DEVELOPMENT

While writing the cover letter, you should address as many of the requirements for the job position as possible. It is important to use real-life examples while stating your qualifications. In other words, do not just say you are the most reliable person for the position, demonstrate this quality with an actual instance to prove so.

Most important, in this letter you will prove to the reader that you meet the requirements posted in the job description that you wrote down in the above section. You may not have actual job experience to meet one of the requirements, yet you could have taken a course or had an opportunity to perform something similar at a previous job you held. For example, if you are applying for a computer software job that requires C++ programming skills, you could meet that requirement by demonstrating a project you have completed on your own that required that language or a class you have taken.

Again, you will be judged the best candidate for the position by how well you are able to convince the reader of your ability to carry out the requirements of the job through your experience and education.

PEER REVIEW

Exchange your assignment with another student. Let them tell you how well you addressed the requirements of the job you are applying for by relating the strengths of your argument in the cover letter. They can also read your resume to see if your experience and education would qualify you for the position.

Learn from the suggestions from your peers as well as from your mistakes. The things you will remember the most are the corrections to your mistakes.

VOCABULARY

Lorem ipsum
persuasive
quadrant
soft break

CHAPTER THREE

Applying Styles to a Document

Estimated time to complete: 20–30 minutes

INTRODUCTION

Styles are applied to documents for many different reasons. In this chapter you will see how styles affect the organization of a document by applying a unique look to the headings and captions.

PROJECT OVERVIEW

As readers start a scan of a document, they can easily understand the organization of the material by the types of headings. To many companies, the style of their documents reflects their corporate image in the same manner a logo does.

One reason to add styles to your written work is to assist readers in understanding the many sections of the document. By organizing your writing into different classes or headings, it becomes clear to the reader which sections are the main headings and which are subheadings. This look can be achieved in several ways.

PROJECT DESIGN

In information technology, a boilerplate is a unit of writing that can be reused over and over without change. In computer programming, boilerplate code or boilerplate refers to sections of code that repeat in many places.

Boilerplate is a term that refers to a standardized document, method, or procedure. In the field of law, boilerplate documents

SIDE BOX 3.1:
Boilerplate Elements

Many companies have established a certain look to all their corporate communications. This would include such items as fonts, margins, corporate colors, and logos. These items are often referred to as boilerplate designs. Rules often govern the use of reusable elements such as logos, often limiting their use to specific sizes, colors, and documents. Text that is often repeated, such as the corporate mission statement, can be copied and pasted word for word by authorized employees.

are commonly used for efficiency and to increase standardization in the structure and language of legal documents, such as contracts, investment prospectuses, and bond indentures.

Hundreds of different options are available to you in applying styles to your document. Each section of your document can easily be identified by the unique style you have applied to it. You should also consider how you would label your images, charts, and tables so that they are easy for the reader to identify. In this exercise you will use your word processing software to apply unique styles to headings, captions, and other major designs. Then you will generate a Table of Contents (TOC) and a Table of Figures for your paper.

For this assignment, you will stylize the following key elements:

- Title
- Heading 1
- Heading 2
- Heading 3
- Captions
- Direct quotes

By applying font sizes consistently you can establish the importance of each of these items. You could possibly use larger fonts for the main divisions and smaller ones for subdivisions.

PROJECT DEVELOPMENT

In this project you are to apply the boilerplate elements of your company to a product literature catalog. You may need to change the default settings in your word processor program by going to the Styles section located in the ribbon at the top of your program. There are very strict formatting guides describing specific styles, and each of these styles must be applied to this document using the following information:

- Margins: 1" top, bottom, and right; 1.25" left
- Title: Times New Roman, 28 point (pt), center justified, small caps
- Normal text: Times New Roman, 12 pt, left justified
- H1 (heading 1): Times New Roman 18 pt, bold, left justified, 6 pts before, 6 pts after
- H2 (heading 2): Times New Roman, 14 pt bold, 6 pts before, 6 pts after, left indent 0.50"
- H3 (heading 3): Times New Roman, 12 pt bold, 2 pts before, 2 pts after, left indent 0.80"
- Caption (text under your images): Times New Roman, 10 pt italic, center (under image)
- Quote: Times New Roman, 10 pt italic, left align, left indent 0.7", right indent 0.7", 10 pts before, 8 pts after

Once you have all your headings and captions properly marked, you can generate a Table of Contents (TOC). Your word processing program will scan through all your headings and automatically set up a Table of Contents based on the styles you have attributed to each of your headings. Do not worry if this needs to be changed in the future, as there is an *update* command available to you.

PEER REVIEW

After you have designed your document by clearly marking each of the major sections, have a classmate review your work to evaluate the design in terms of visual appeal and visual rhetoric. The visual rhetoric of your design is the underlying meaning the reader perceives while reading your paper. Are each of the sections easy to identify? Are all the pictures, charts, and tables properly identified? The answers to these questions should give you an idea of the quality of the paper's overall organization.

The better the paper looks, the more credible your writing becomes. This is important in any paper especially if you are trying to convince someone to your way of thinking.

CSS STYLES

Styles are used in many websites by using a technology called CSS Styles. These work the same way as the styles used in your office software. Once the style or look of your website is established, all your work can be saved in simple files called Cascading Style Sheets (CSS).

Many characteristics of your website can be saved to this single file with a .css extension (such as a file named *styles.css*) or embedded into each page of your website individually. This would include font choice, page colors, sections, background colors or images, and much more.

If you wish to develop a website, many online sources, called content management systems (CMS), are available to assist you in this endeavor. Some of the more popular open source systems are Joomla, WordPress, Drupal, and Mambo. You can quickly set up the entire look to your website, ensuring uniformity throughout.

VOCABULARY

boilerplate
cascading
rhetoric

CHAPTER FOUR

Constructing Tables

Estimated time to complete: 20–30 minutes

INTRODUCTION

A simple way to clarify information in a document is by placing the information in a table. This allows the reader to easily compare your findings by placing information in a logical sequence. In this chapter, you will learn table structure and the importance of visual communication when using them.

PROJECT OVERVIEW

In the second part of this project you will construct a table from information extracted from a set of paragraphs.

PROJECT DESIGN

To understand the structure of a table, it is necessary to review the different sections.

Title is at the top →

Heading names at → top of each column

Rows contain information for each specific item.

TABLE 4.1   *Crop Review for Ohio in 2017*

CROP NAME	ACRES PLANTED	PRICE/ BUSHEL	TOTAL CROP VALUE
Soybean	5,100,000	9.50	2,393,573,000
Corn	3,400,000	3.55	1,966,736,000
Wheat	460,000	4.90	157,731,000
Oats	60,000	3.50	4,900,000

Note: Prices in US Dollars (USD).

Columns

Title: The title always appears at the top of the table. It can be placed on the top of the table or within its own row. This is the opposite of identifying an image or picture used in your paper. The identifier for an image or picture is placed underneath.

Headings: These should clearly mark the type of information included in the columns below them, so the reader can make comparisons to each item.

Columns: Up and down. Notice that all numerical figures are aligned on the right so that the decimal place would be considered in the same position for each entry. Try to keep all numbers to the same decimal place.

Rows: Across. This is the same information as you would find in the record of a database. In other words, all the information on the lines going across pertain to the first item on the left.

Table 4.2 contains many mistakes in grammar, alignment, and construction. For this exercise, you will mark the mistakes as they appear in the table. Try to find as many as you can.

TABLE 4.2 *Results of students declaring majors*

I WANT TO MAJOR IN	UPPER CLASSMEN		FRESHMAN STUDENTS	
	FIRST DAY	2ND DAY	FIRST DAY	DAY 2
NUMBER	520	48.0	555	41,10
Engineering	43.2	37	38.00	41
Biology	25	23	25	20
Mathomatics	12	30.0	27	30
IDK	20	10	10.0	9
	100.00%	100	100 percent	100%

PROJECT DEVELOPMENT

The following paragraph contains a lot of technical data. While reading it, the user might have a difficult time comparing the different values of the different items being described. By extracting the data from the paragraph and placing it in a table, you provide a clear, visual interpretation for the reader.

SCENARIO

You are an automotive engineer at Viking Brake Pad Incorporated. Marketing has asked for a comparison of its new ceramic brake pad, the Viking Ceramo ST, to an existing metallic pad, the Viking Metallica.

You have compiled the following information and must present it to your colleagues in a way that is clear and easy to understand. You decide to place the information in an easy-to-read table.

Viking Ceramo ST, Ceramic Brake Pads

Pros: They're quieter than metallic pads. They dissipate heat better for less brake fade. They create less dust, and the dust itself is lighter in color. They're gentler on brake rotors.

Cons: They're not as aggressive as metallic pads. They're not recommended for racing or heavy-duty towing. They're generally more expensive than comparable metallic pads. Website customers have rated these 4-1/2 out of 5 stars. They come with a 90-day warranty at the cost of $57.95 a pair. They are considered a good choice for everyday driving.

Ars Metallica, Metallic Brake Pads

As their name implies, metallic pads are made with metal fibers in the braking compound ... and, they're fun to listen to while you drive. Here are the pros and cons of metallic brake pads that you have discovered:

Pros: They're more aggressive than ceramic pads yet they pull heat away from the rotor for cooler braking. They're available in track-ready and heavy-duty towing formulations. They're relatively less expensive than comparable ceramic pads.

Cons: They're louder than ceramic pads. They generate more dust that's

SIDE BOX 4.1:
Special Notes or Acknowledgments

You may place information at the bottom of a table to help the reader understand the terminology you have used. You may also acknowledge the source of your information at the bottom of the table, such as:

Source: US Department of Agriculture 2017 State Agriculture Review.

or

NOTE: All figures are represented in tons of grain.

black and grimy. They're more abrasive and wear through disc brakes faster. They have a lower customer rating of 3-1/2 out of 5 stars. They are known for extended wear and high dust. The pads have a lifetime warranty and cost $43.95 a pair. They come highly recommended for use in muscle cars. Some consumers like them as they make a high screeching sound during breaking.

Create your table in this space:

PEER REVIEW

Compare how many mistakes you found in Table 4.2 with others in the class. There may be more than 20 mistakes that you could possibly find in the exercise.

When gathering information from a paragraph to place inside a table, be sure everything is ordered in a logical manner to avoid confusion.

VOCABULARY

agriculture
colleagues
extract
formulations
identifier
scenario

REFERENCE

https://www.nass.usda.gov/Quick_Stats/Ag_Overview/state-
  Overview.php?state=OHIO

CHAPTER FIVE

Understanding Graphic Formats

Estimated time to complete: 20–30 minutes

INTRODUCTION

In this exercise, you will learn the importance of using the correct graphic image for the type of communication you are using. Images used in print documents require a different format than those used for presentation on a computer screen or smartphone. You will inspect the resolution of an image, its color palette, and the type of file name used to save it. You will also distinguish between RGB and CMYK color palettes.

PROJECT OVERVIEW

You will explore the two main families of graphics: bitmap images (often called raster images) and vector images. An understanding of graphics also requires knowledge of color palettes and which one to use based on a document's end use.

Raster and Vector Graphics

The two basic families of images are raster (bitmap) and vector. At first glance the two appear very similar, but on closer look you will see that their makeup differs.

FIGURE 5.1   Raster or vector images?

A raster image consists of tiny blocks of colors (or grays) called *pixels*. If you were to zoom in or magnify the raster image you would see the pixels (see Figure 5.2).[1] These tiny blocks can be defined in quality by the number of dots (pixels) per inch. The more pixels per inch, the better the viewing or print quality. If you were to double the image size to make it look bigger, you would still have the same number of dots or pixels, but they would cover twice the area and look very blurry.

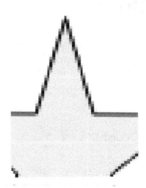

FIGURE 5.2   Closeup of a raster image.

---

1   J. W. Peterson and Adobe Systems Incorporated. 2008. "Distortion of raster and vector artwork." US Patent 8,760,467, filed May 20, 2008, and issued June 24, 2014.

Some common types of raster images and their file extensions are:

JPEG or JPG: Acronym for Joint Photographic Experts Group. Pronounced "jay-peg." Contains millions of colors, so it works best with photographs or artwork.

GIF: Acronym for Graphics Interchange Format. Pronounced "giff" or "jiff." Uses 256 colors to represent an entire image. Can be animated with a sequence of images contained in one file. Can be used in Microsoft Office applications and websites.

PNG: Acronym for Portable Network Graphics. Pronounced "peeng." Similar to a JPEG in that it contains millions of colors, but it allows editing of text entries.

BMP: A Windows bitmap file that is similar to a GIF file. Can be used in PowerPoint and other Microsoft Office programs like Word. Not suggested for websites.

TIFF: Acronym for Tagged Information File Format. The more dots or pixels per inch, the larger the file. Commonly used in printing, but the files can become quite large because 300 to 1,200 dots per inch (DPI) are needed to ensure a quality printout.

Vector images are useful because you can double the size of an image and it will maintain its original quality without any blurriness. Vector images are not defined by tiny pixels but rather by a mathematical ratio explaining their lines and fills inside the image. Therefore, if you were to double the size of the image, the size of all the fill areas and lines would double as well. This maintains the clarity of the image no matter how large you make it.

Some common types of vector graphics and their extensions are:

EPS: Acronym for Encapsulated PostScript. Can contain text and an image.

DXF/DWG: Often used in AutoCAD™ and other engineering drawings.

SVG: Acronym for Scalable Vector Graphic.

RGB or CMYK? The Two Main Color Palettes

How you plan on using an image will determine which color palette you will use. In general, files viewed on a computer screen should be created using the RGB palette, which simply stands for red, green, and blue. Files that are to be printed on paper tend to use the CMYK palette. The palette name represents the early color plates used in printing: cyan, magenta, yellow, and key (black).[2]

RGB

Your computer screen consists of three layers that emit light and represent the three colors of red, green, and blue. By combining these overlapping colors, we can represent millions of new colors on the computer screen.

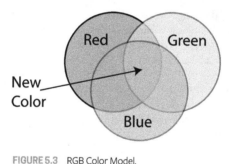

FIGURE 5.3   RGB Color Model.

It follows the same theory as painting one color over another to achieve a new third color. If you painted red over blue, then you would produce purple.[3]

CMYK

To produce a graphic image for a high-end printer we need to add a fourth screen or plate. In the CMYK palette we have four colors

---

2   B. Stukenborg, M. Witkowski, and D. McGavin, "Color Figures in BJ: RGB versus CMYK," *Biophysical Journal* 88m no. 2 (2005): 761–762.

3   A. A. Alshammari, "Web-Based Computer Graphics Learning" (master's thesis, University of Cincinnati, 2018).

representing the colors cyan, magenta, yellow, and black (or key). Paper produces an image the exact opposite way as a computer screen does. Instead of emitting light to produce colors, paper *reflects* light and needs to be represented by printing four different times over the same piece of paper. Cyan is a blue color, magenta is a reddish color, and yellow and black are the original colors.

If the wrong type of file is submitted, then the ink printer will not operate. A very common mistake is expecting a three-color RGB file to print on a CMYK ink printer.

Figure 5.4 depicts the same piece of paper being printed four different times. Each time the paper is printed a different color of ink is absorbed into the paper to form the final image based on all four CMYK colors.

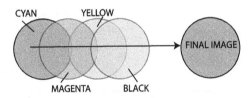

FIGURE 5.4   CMYK Model.

PROJECT DESIGN

In this project you will create your own logo. After you create the logo, you must decide the file format that would be best for your project. You can export your final file to one of the many different file types. You can base your design on a fictitious business or something you always wanted to create.

PROJECT DEVELOPMENT

First, select the software you will use to create the logo. If you would like to use open source (i.e., free) software, try one of these:

- InkScape©: This is an open source drawing program similar to Adobe Illustrator© that will create drawings in a vector format and then allow you to export them to either CMYK or RGB format for use in your project. It also allows you to export vector or raster file types such as PNG, OpenDocument Drawing, DXF, sk1, PDF, EPS, and PostScript. It provides useful tutorials to get you started.

- GIMP: The GNU Image Manipulation Program, or GIMP, is similar to Adobe Photoshop© and allows you to create drawings in RGB raster format. It also allows you to export to CMYK format by a process called "stripping the layers," which is explained on its website. There is also a section of tutorials to assist you.

It is also possible to use PowerPoint to create your logo. Once you are finished with your design, export it to a PNG, JPEG, GIF, or BMP file.

Once you are familiar with the software you have chosen to use, design a logo for your personal use. The final use of your logo will determine the type of file you will export the file to. You will prepare two different files of your logo: one for print and one for computer screen.

For anything viewed on a computer screen (i.e., images used in PowerPoint, websites, and so forth), you could select an RGB color format, then export to PNG, JPEG, GIF, or BMP (if used in Microsoft Office or Open Office). The resolution should be low, such as 72 or 96 dpi. This will keep the size of the file down for easy handling and transport.

If you are to provide a print bureau a file to be used in four-color printing, such as a magazine, book, or journal, you could use the CMYK palette and then export the image to either an EPS or TIFF file. The EPS is much smaller in size because it is a vector file. The TIFF file is quite large, as you need to have an image at least 300 dpi.

FIGURE 5.5 My Logo.

PEER REVIEW

Have a fellow student check the quality of your drawing for originality, complexity, and proper format.

VOCABULARY

dots per inch (dpi)
CMYK palette
raster
RGB palette
vector

CHAPTER SIX

Writing a Product Specification Sheet

Estimated time to complete: 20–30 minutes

INTRODUCTION

A product specification sheet is a type of document you would receive when comparing different products based on the qualities they possess. These are typically used at tradeshows as handouts so that buyers can compare different products. These sheets are not instruction manuals; they do not inform the user on the operation of the object, but rather its capabilities.

FIGURE 6.1   Product Specification Sample.

PROJECT OVERVIEW

In this project you will create a product specification sheet using materials and information from previous projects. You will create a one-page document that provides the following:

- A large table to hold all your product information
- An image suitable for printing
- A QR Code

QR Codes are very useful in storing information that can be obtained by scanning them with the camera on a smartphone or tablet. They can hold up to 100 times more data than a conventional barcode and many different types of information. Some of the more common types of information stored in QR Codes are:

- Website URL: Links to external websites
- VCard: Virtual business cards
- Text: Simple text messages
- SMS: Short Message Service smartphone messages
- Facebook: Facebook page links
- App store: Link to an app in an app store
- PDF files: Files of catalogs or other documents

PROJECT DESIGN

For this project you will select an object of your choice to be displayed on a printed sheet of paper, typically one used at a tradeshow or other sales event. By using a table, you will be able to control the positioning of the elements to create a balanced, easy-to-read product specification sheet.
Within the table you will insert:

1. A graphic image suitable for printing
2. A QR Code containing a message of your choice
3. Text explaining the capabilities or qualities of the object you have selected

The QR Code is very useful when designing a product specification sheet. It can provide the user with updated pricing, specifications, or contact information that may be subject to change without reprinting the entire sheet.

FIGURE 6.2   QR Code.

PROJECT DEVELOPMENT

Decide how the table should look before you create it. You can start with any number of rows and columns and then merge or add cells to construct your design.

Many different websites and apps are available to create QR Codes. Once you select the tool you are going to use to create the QR Code, decide on the type of information you would like to embed in that code. Import the QR Code into the table by selecting the cell of the table where it should be placed. Do the same for an image of a product you would like to place in your sheet. When importing images into a table, it is easy to distort the images when you reduce or enlarge them. The secret is to hold down the Shift key while you push up and diagonally on the lower-right selector (Figure 6.3). This will change the size of the image proportionally.

Hold <shift> key and push up diagonally.

FIGURE 6.3   Changing image size.

PEER REVIEW

Have another student review your work. The images should not be distorted, especially the QR Code, or it may not scan properly. The information regarding the product should explain the features or capabilities of the item. The whole idea of the product specification sheet is to present an opportunity for shoppers to compare this product with other similar ones. It does not explain how to operate the item in any way. The QR Code should present additional material that may not be available at the time of printing.

VOCABULARY

proportionally
QR Code
SMS
VCard

Figure Credits
Figure 6.2: Source: https://www.qrcode-monkey.com/.

Constructing an Instruction Manual

Estimated time to complete: 20–30 minutes

INTRODUCTION

In this chapter, you will write an instruction manual that conveys to the reader all the information they will need to successfully complete a project. The style of writing for this task is very different from that used with the other documents you have previously created. Your goal is to provide directions to complete an activity, heading off any possible user mistakes along the way.

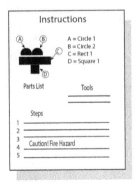

FIGURE 7.1   Instructions Sample.

PROJECT OVERVIEW

The instruction manual is designed to reduce the number of possible user mistakes. You must be able to foresee any flaws in the design or possible mistakes the user could make. You want your audience to be able to complete the project without ruining it or injuring themselves.

PROJECT DESIGN

Your instruction sheet should include the following:

1. An introduction that clearly states the expected outcome.
   - State the intended audience and whether a novice or an experienced tradesman would be capable of completing the task.
   - Give an estimate as to the time it would take to complete the project.
2. Equipment and supplies needed to complete the operation.
   - Identify the tools needed to complete the project (e.g., hammer, saw, screwdriver, etc.).
   - Note if certain items are not supplied with the project (e.g., batteries, glue, screws, etc.).
3. Step-by-step instructions.
   - Make sure your steps are in the proper order so users do not ruin the project or injure themselves.
   - The instructions should be commands, not suggestions. The imperative style of writing is suggested.
   - Let your users know exactly why they are doing certain steps by providing a bit of background information.
4. Recommendations and warnings.
   - As the project proceeds, you should interject with captions that would describe the importance of completing certain steps to avoid ruining the project or worse, injuring the user.
   - Typically, words like *caution*, *attention*, and *danger* are used depending on the possible consequences.
5. Images.
   - As always, a picture is worth a thousand words, especially a picture that shows exactly how to assemble different parts of the project or that labels the name of each part to avoid confusion.

- Try to show smaller portions of the item to zoom in on the task at hand.
- Search for and use any symbol necessary to depict warnings for hazards such as *fire*, *laser*, *chemical*, *corrosive*, etc.

PROJECT DEVELOPMENT

You are to create an instruction sheet with complete step-by-step instructions, warnings, images, and any other information needed to complete a project of your choosing. Your project could be on how to assemble an item, cook a recipe, use new software, fix an appliance, and so on. You must be able to foresee any possible mistakes users would make in the process and help them avoid them.

PEER REVIEW

After you have completed your instruction manual, have another student verify the steps you have written to ensure that the project could be successfully created without mistake or injury. It is difficult to predict how another person may misuse different parts during assembly. It is always important to evaluate your work before it is published to avoid possible confusion.

VOCABULARY

imperative voice
novice
tradesman

CHAPTER EIGHT

Designing Quad Charts

Estimated time to complete: 20–30 minutes

INTRODUCTION

Before full proposals are accepted for grants, institutions or companies may require you to submit a condensed version of your idea on a single sheet of paper, divided into four essential sections, called a *quad chart*. If your idea is accepted, you may then be invited to submit a full proposal to the grantor. This saves the team reviewing proposals a lot of time because they can learn a lot about an idea from a well-formed quad chart. In this exercise, you construct a quad chart based on one of several available designs.

PROJECT OVERVIEW

You will analyze the potential market for an idea you wish to develop. You can do so by visiting the government website Grants.gov (www.grants.gov), which has thousands of requests from government agencies and other organizations. Both government agencies and large businesses often require submission of a quad chart by potential contractors as part of the contract-bidding process. Some of the more common government agencies that request quad charts are the National Aeronautics and Space Administration (NASA), the Defense Advanced Research Projects Agency (DARPA), and the United States Air Force (USAF). The quad chart is a traditional one-page summary of a project. It asks for a brief description of the project, a statement about the potential benefit from the project, a description of the management approach for the project, and a summary of the cost and schedule for the project.[1]

---

1   "Instructions for Building an Entry Quad Chart," NASA website, PowerPoint, EntryQuad_instructions_template.pptx, viewed September 2018.

PROJECT DESIGN

Several important components are included in most quad charts. You will investigate the most common design elements in this project. However, note that you should determine the grantor's exact requirements before you begin, as some agencies require different data in each section or may even request the quad chart to be in portrait orientation.

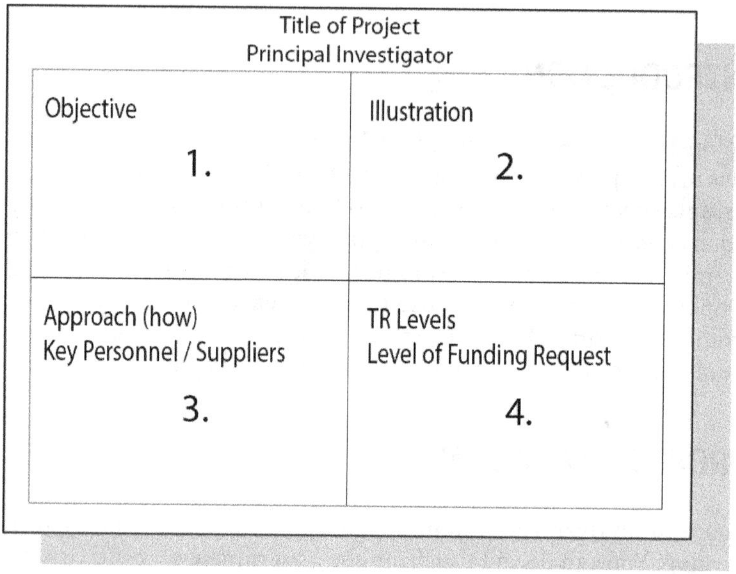

Title of Project Principal Investigator	
Objective 1.	Illustration 2.
Approach (how) Key Personnel / Suppliers 3.	TR Levels Level of Funding Request 4.

FIGURE 8.1 Quad Chart Sections.

Most of the time the quad chart will be printed in landscape orientation. At the very top you should give your project a memorable title and then list the principal investigator (PI), who is usually the head of the laboratory or a research group leader. Each quadrant has a specific type of information that is requested from the grantor:

1. **Top-left quadrant:** The objective ("what" the task will do) in bullet format.
2. **Top-right quadrant:** A representative illustration of the technology at the initial stage of the task.

3. **Bottom-left quadrant:** The approach, which is "how," in bullet form, the task will be accomplished. You may add the materials used and the source of the materials from various vendors. This quadrant also lists any *CoPIs/Partners* (a *Co-PI* is another way of saying there are other principal investigators).

4. **Bottom-right quadrant:** Using technology readiness levels (TRLs), indicate your major accomplishments thus far. The nine levels are listed below, and you will observe that the higher the rating, the more likely you are to receive funding. A working prototype is far more appealing than a good idea.

The nine TRL milestones are as follows:

Level 1. You have a basic idea that you have observed and believe is worth of funding.

Level 2. You have properly defined your concept along scientific guidelines.

Level 3. The idea has been proven through accepted lab techniques.

Level 4. You have validated parts such as breadboards and other smaller components.

Level 5. Demonstration of components completed in a relevant environment.

Level 6. Demonstration of prototype completed in a relevant environment.

Level 7. Demonstration of prototype achieved in a space environment.

Level 8. Project completed and tested in ground or space environments.

Level 9. Used in flight missions and proved effective.

PROJECT DEVELOPMENT

Writing assignment for today's session.

Create your quad chart in landscape orientation based on the following information.

- In the top section give your idea a memorable title; it will help people remember the idea.
- You are the Principal Investigator (PI). Others that are involved in the project are usually referred to as CoPIs.
- Fill each of the quadrants with the required information. If you do not have an idea of your own, you may use this one:
  - This project proposal is requesting $100,000 to develop the magnetic widget bearing. This item will reduce wear on conventional ball bearings by eliminating the magnetic frequency among all the parts in one basket. It does so by spinning the bearings around a central axis. This prolongs bearing life in electric motors.
  - Use your imagination and draw your own picture of what this item might look like. Add an accompanying breadboard.
  - All the parts for assembly were purchased at Acme Inc. of New Philadelphia, Ohio.
  - You are assisted in the laboratory by Jane Dougherty, PhD and your intern Ralph Jergenson. You have created this object based on an improvement to the existing research you created on magnetic flux of bearings in motors. The quad chart was created on September 20, 2018.
  - You have demonstrated a working prototype and tested it in a space environment, yet you need the grant to set up production on a large scale as of today. (What TR Level would this be?) Previous milestones are as follows:

1. Requirements, structure, architecture   06/15
2. Breadboard demo (TRL 5)   08/16
3. Build with integrated calibrator   02/17
4. Prototype validation   08/17

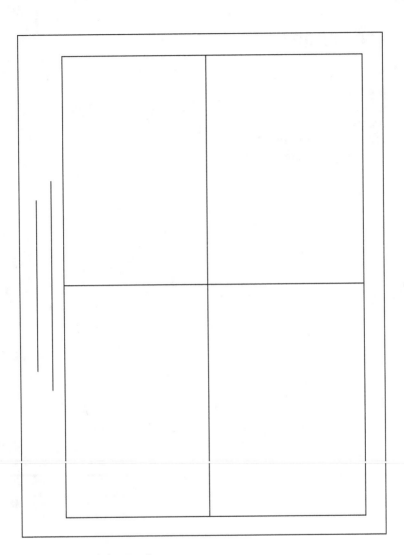

FIGURE 8.2 Quad Chart Template

PEER REVIEW

Have another student evaluate your work based on the sections you have developed in the exercise. Each quadrant in the chart should represent a specific type of information.

Learn from the suggestions from your peers as well as from your mistakes. The things you will remember the most are the corrections to your mistakes.

VOCABULARY

breadboard
grantor
milestone
prototype
request for proposal (RFP)
technology readiness levels (TRLs)

CHAPTER NINE

Formulating Convincing Lab Reports

Estimated time to complete: 50–60 minutes

INTRODUCTION

In this chapter, you will write a lab report that reports the results of your research to some other department at work, or possibly another company or organization altogether. Seven different scenarios are provided. You may select the one that most interests you based on your field of study.

PROJECT OVERVIEW

The lab report is designed to persuade the reader to your way of thinking by providing accurate test results. It is also used to finalize the hypotheses you have constructed through scientific research. You can simulate the findings through facts provided in journals, books, websites, and possibly data from subject matter experts (SMEs). Your information must be convincing enough to impress the reader to agree with and follow your final decision.

You should also include a specific design for your research and how it was conducted so that other investigators could take your work and achieve the same results.

PROJECT DESIGN

Your lab report should have the following headings:

1. **Introduction:** Inform the reader of the background leading up to this research.
2. **Your Research:** There will likely be many new terms and procedures that you must research before you begin the experiment. Inform the reader of any journals, books, or websites you used to understand the problem at hand before you began testing.
3. **Basis of Your Experiment:** You have decided to implement certain equipment and procedures for your testing. The reader should be able to reenact your experiment by using the same procedures under the same environmental conditions and get the same results that you did.
4. **Results of Your Experiment:** Place all your findings in an easy-to-read comparison table (see Table 9.1). This will give the reader of your report a clear way to review your findings with an easy-to-read graphic or chart. The results should provide enough evidence to convince your reader that your testing provided the best solution.

TABLE 9.1 *Comparison of findings*

TEST ITEMS	TEST #1	TEST #2	TEST #3
ITEM 1			
ITEM 2			
ITEM 3			

5. **Conclusions:** Draw conclusions based on the data you have entered in your table and explain how you arrived at them.
6. **Future Research:** Try to leave your research and testing open to further work. You may have found an interesting development in your testing that was not expected. This could lead to extended research on this topic or even a new investigation in another field.

7. **References:** This will be a complete list of information sources used in this report. This would any books, interviews, emails, and other preliminary research into the subject matter.

PROJECT DEVELOPMENT

You are now ready to write your lab report.

Seven different topics for lab reports are listed below. Pick the one that most interests you and follow the suggested outline in the Project Design section.

Scenario 1

Hot Pepper Sauces

You are a chemical engineer at Pepper's Hot Sauce Company in Dallas, Texas. Marketing has asked for a formula improvement to its existing hot sauce, the Blazing Inferno. The new sauce will be called Take No Prisoners. Marketing would like this new sauce to be hotter than any of the competition. You must provide the following information:

1. The Scoville heat units (SHUs) for the existing Blazing Inferno sauce based on the Scoville scale.
2. The SHUs for two competitors' sauces of your choice (e.g., Original Beer Barrel Embalming Fluid).

The Scoville scale is a measurement of the pungency (spicy heat) of chili peppers—such as the jalapeño, the bhut jolokia, and the world's current hottest pepper, the Carolina Reaper—or other spicy foods that is based on capsaicin concentration. The Red Savina pepper, one of the hottest chilies, is rated at around 500,000 SHUs. The bhut jolokia (ghost pepper) is rated at over 1 million SHUs. The following peppers have SHUs of 855,000 to 2,200,000: Komodo Dragon, Trinidad Moruga Scorpion, Naga Viper, Infinity Chili, Naga Morich, Bhut jolokia (ghost pepper), Trinidad Scorpion Butch T, Bedfordshire Super Naga, Spanish Naga Chili, and the Carolina Reaper.

You have compiled the following information and must present it in a lab report with tables and pictures. You include your research on the competitors' products as well.

1. You have created a list of the hottest peppers known to man for consideration in your formula for Take No Prisoners. You will select three of these to use in the Take No Prisoners formula, showing the Scoville rating.
2. You have created a table comparing two of your largest competitors to the old Blazing Inferno formula and the new Take No Prisoners formula. The table includes each product's Scoville rating, price per bottle, and number of bottles sold worldwide.
3. You suggest the warning label to be used on the bottle of Take No Prisoners.

Scenario 2

Brake Pad Comparison

You are an automotive engineer at Acme Brake Pad Incorporated. Marketing has asked for a comparison of its new ceramic brake bad, the Acme Ceramo ST, with an existing metallic pad, the Acme Metallica.

You have compiled the following information and must present it in a lab report with tables and pictures. You also include research you have found from competitors.

Acme Ceramo ST, Ceramic Brake Pads

Pros: They're quieter than metallic pads. They dissipate heat better for less brake fade. They create less dust, and the dust itself is lighter in color. They're gentler on brake rotors.

Cons: They're not as aggressive as metallic pads. They're not recommended for racing or heavy-duty towing. They're generally more expensive than comparable metallic pads.

- Customer rating of 4-1/2 stars
- Extended wear, low dust
- 90-day warranty
- $57.95 a pair

- Good for everyday driving
- Low noise

Acme Metallica, Metallic Brake Pads

As their name implies, metallic pads are made with metal fibers in the braking compound, and they're fun to listen to while you drive.

Pros: They're more aggressive than ceramic pads. They pull heat away from the rotor for cooler braking. They're available in track-ready and heavy-duty towing formulations. They're relatively less expensive than comparable ceramic pads.

Cons: They're louder than ceramic pads. They generate more dust that's black and grimy. They're more abrasive and wear through disc brakes faster.

- Customer rating of 3-1/2 stars
- Extended wear, high dust
- Lifetime warranty
- $43.95 a pair
- Recommended use for muscle cars
- High screech sound during breaking

Scenario 3

Drones for Bridge Inspections

You are a civil engineer at the Minnesota Department of Transportation (MnDOT). Seeing the potential of unmanned aerial vehicles (UAVs) to aid in bridge inspections, MnDOT has requested a demonstration project to evaluate the technology, safety, cost, and effectiveness of UAVs for bridge inspection compared to current methods.

You have been asked to compare several UAVs (i.e., drones) used for bridge inspections.

Bridges were selected based on the following factors:

1. Cooperation of local agency
2. Safety
3. Varied bridge types and sizes

4. Location
5. FAA requirements

The four bridges are as follows:

1. Bridge 13509, Chisago County, prestressed beam bridge
2. Bridge 448, Oronoco, concrete arch
3. Bridge 49553, Little Falls, pedestrian steel deck truss
4. Arcola RR Bridge, Stillwater, high steel arch railroad bridge

You have compiled the following information and must present it in a lab report with tables and pictures.

Study 1: Aeryon Skyranger
For this study, an Aeyron Skyranger UAV (Skyranger) was used. This aircraft was designed with military, public safety, and commercial use in mind. The Skyranger is a very robust and capable unit and offered several advantages for this study. The all-weather ability allowed us to work in the rain, which occurred within the first two days of field work. The Skyranger can change payloads to utilize a standard camera, an optical zoom camera, and an infrared camera. The Skyranger also has a very long battery life at around 50 minutes. While the Skyranger met many of the requirements for collecting inspection data, it did not have the ability to look upward. Therefore, a 360-degree video camera was installed on top of the Skyranger, but due to Wi-Fi signal interference it did not perform correctly. In addition, the Skyranger did not have the ability to fly under the bridge decks because loss of the GPS signal would cause the aircraft to fly vertically and return to the launch point; which was problematic with a bridge deck overhead.
    The purchase cost for the Skyranger unit is approximately $140,000.

Study 2: SenseFly Albris
The SenseFly Albris provides submillimeter image resolution using a safe, lightweight system. It can capture and geotag video, still, and thermal imagery, all during the same flight, without landing to change cameras. The SenseFly can be used in autonomous, GPS-guided mode or via the ScreenFly feature

to observe structures and surfaces live, in real time. The cost is about $80,000.

Study 3: Skycatch Evolution 3, a Lower-Cost UAV
The original fieldwork included utilizing different UAV models as a comparison between technologies. Although exemptions for several models were submitted to the FAA, none were approved in time for the field work portion of this project phase. There are many UAVs currently on the market with GPS and imaging capability starting at around $1,000. The wide range in price is attributed to features and length of battery life.

The battery on a lower-cost UAV may only last 10 to 20 minutes, whereas the battery in a higher-end UAV will typically last close to 60 minutes. Lower-end models typically lack postprocessing software, failsafe modes, and have lower material and build quality, making them less suitable as a tool for bridge inspection. The costs and features available on UAVs is changing rapidly as the technology advances.

Study 4: Current Inspection Method
Workers are forced to climb as close as possible to view the underside of structures and evaluate damage from rust, corrosion, and other weather-related activity. There is also the possibility of damage from heavy payloads on the deck of the bridge from constant use.

Scenario 4

Concrete Resistance
Your university has just received a grant from the Ohio Department of Transportation (ODOT) to investigate ways to make road concrete more resistant to winter salt applications. Your research has shown that the ancient Romans had great success in making concrete that is resistant to seawater, which has a high saline content. So, what did the Romans know that we don't?[1]

---

1   M. Crawford, "Ancient Roman Concrete Stands the Test of Time," ASME.org, September 7, 2017, https://www.asme.org/ engineering-topics/articles/technology-and-society/ancient-roman-concrete-stands-test-time. Viewed October 14, 2017.

Roman structures still stand—buildings, bridges, arches, roads, piers, and breakwaters—thanks in large part to the concrete and mortar that the Roman engineers designed. Amazingly, even in corrosive saltwater environments, Roman concrete harbor structures have remained strong and intact for more than 2,000 years. Compare this spectacular longevity to modern-day Portland cement, which, even when reinforced with rebar, might last 100 years in a marine environment.

The Romans made concrete by combining lime with volcanic ash to make a mortar and then mixing in fragments of volcanic rock (the aggregate). This material was used to build many impressive structures, including the Pantheon and Trajan's Market in Rome, as well as large-scale piers and breakwaters along the coastline designed to protect busy shipping harbors.

"We can go into the tiny natural laboratories in the concrete, map the minerals that are present, the succession of the crystals that occur, and their crystallographic properties," said researcher Marie Jackson of Berkeley.[2] A team of researchers was surprised to discover high concentrations of zeolite, phillipsite, and tobermorite occupying the porous spaces in the concrete, many of them created by the dissolution of other minerals, such as feldspar.

Jackson theorizes that the steady percolation of seawater into the Roman concrete reacted with the lime and the volcanic ash to create these interlocking minerals that occupied void space, making the concrete stronger. The long, platelike crystals of tobermorite also created an unusual flexibility within the submerged concrete that increased with time.

In contrast, anticorrosive Portland cement mixes are formulated to be inert and unreactive with seawater yet start to deteriorate far earlier. "Contrary to the principles of modern cement-based concrete," Jackson said, "the Romans created a rock-like concrete that thrives in open chemical exchange with seawater."

A modern equivalent of Roman concrete would be ideal for seawall structures and other marine applications, as well as for encasing high-level wastes in cement-like barriers that protect the surrounding environment. Widespread use of this concrete

---

2   M. D. Jackson, S. R. Mulcahy, H. Chen, Y. Li, Q. Li, P. Cappelletti, and H.-R. Wenk, "Phillipsite and Al-Tobermorite Mineral Cements Produced Through Low-Temperature Water–Rock Reactions in Roman Marine Concrete," ASME.org, July 2017, https://www.asme.org/engineering-topics/articles/arctic-engineering/wind-turbines-whirling-arctic-regions.

would also reduce the construction industry's dependence on Portland cement, the manufacture of which requires high-temperature kilns that emit significant amounts of carbon dioxide.

Your assignment: Research and compare the qualities of ancient Roman concrete to those currently being used and show how the newer products can be improved.

Scenario 5

Wind Turbines Whirling in the Arctic Regions

A telecommunications company providing mobile services in Scandinavia is readying a combination of systems using solar and wind power to replace its costly diesel-powered system. The company began exploring alternative forms of energy because its 20-year-old system was supported by an unreliable grid in a very remote location in northern Norway, and delivery of diesel fuel was becoming increasingly expensive. About six months ago, installation started on a distributed renewable energy solution as a replacement, consisting of one off-grid Urban Green Energy (UGE-600) wind turbine, called the "eddy," and panels providing about 400W of solar energy.

The company is not alone in turning to an alternative to traditional forms of energy. Many companies and remote communities have begun replacing diesel-powered generators with wind and solar power due to both economic and environmental benefits.

Because of the extreme environmental conditions, there are extra steps and testing that must be done, especially for wind energy, because of the moving parts of components. Average temperatures in this Nordic area are below freezing for seven months out of the year, and the average nightly temperature is below 0°F in the winter. Additionally, solar radiation is effectively nonexistent in the winter because there are only about five hours of sunlight. The system is heavily reliant on wind energy during this period.

For installations operating in such harsh environmental conditions, the UGE wind turbines have undergone special testing, including analyses of all components, identification of the right bearing lubrication, and full-scale testing at a commercial cold-testing site in Inner Mongolia, chosen because it is not too far from UGE's manufacturing plant outside of Beijing. Before the full-scale testing, models are created to understand how the brittleness and strength of different materials might be affected under such intense wind loads in cold climates, such as ensuring the structural integrity of steel towers.

"Bearings have proven to be particularly sensitive to temperature fluctuation as temperature decreases to subzero," says Chaskel. Analyzing bearing reaction to cold temperatures involves placing a bearing in a temperature-controlled freezer and allowing the entire component to reach the set point temperature. Parameters for torque and geometric dimensions, for example, are also taken into consideration to determine the best bearing configuration. While a decrease in bearing performance is to be expected in low temperatures, minimizing the effect by optimizing the configuration for durability is the goal. According to Chaskel, "Most important also is the type of lubrication when designing for cold environments. ... The challenge is finding a lubrication type with low viscosity changes and a low freezing point to ensure the turbine continues to operate within the design specification tolerance."

UGE has requested your company test three different lubricants that will meet these specifications. They are expecting your lab report to help them solve this crucial problem.

Scenario 6

Grading Maple Syrup

Your department has received a grant to test methods for producing high-quality maple syrup. Your contact on campus is Debra Jones, PhD, in the Chemical Engineering Department. The company offering the grant to you is West Geauga Sugar Maple of Chardon, Ohio. They would like you to grade and compare their syrup based on data they have found from several competitors.

- Great North Maple
- Ottawa Maple Syrup
- Vermont Sweet Maple

You discover that there are three tools to measure density of maple syrup: the hydrometer, the thermometer, and the refractometer. Density affects syrup quality in several ways. First, syrup must be 66 brix to meet USDA standards, but if it is below 66 brix, it can ferment and cause an off-flavor. Syrup above 67 brix normally does not have an off-flavor, but the higher density can cause crystallization in the bottom of the container and loss of revenue to the producer. What many producers do not realize is that, for a refractometer to work properly, it needs to read a product that is finished and one that is stable in temperature with high clarity.

After some research you have selected a refractometer to measure the liquid. There are many qualities to test in maple syrup. Your department has selected these four as the best control methods for the current project:

- **Density:** Consumers prefer the thicker syrups.
- **Color:** Different shades of amber can also indicate the worth of the product.
- **Clarity:** There are different ratings using letters, such as AA, A, B, and so on.
- **Sugar content (Brix reading using a refractometer):** Make sure the brix number is high enough to ensure a quality product.
- **Packaging:** Proper packaging will aid in the reduction of bacteria in the final product.

SIDE BOX 9.1:
The Brix Scale

The brix scale is used to measure liquids on an instrument called a refractometer. Light passes through a liquid, and the refractometer gives a reading based on the quantity of solids the light passes through. The results of the test are compared to known figures recorded in past readings.

FIGURE 9.1   Refractometer.

Maple syrup boils at 7 degrees above the boiling point of water, or 219°F. Many producers use a thermometer to determine the harvest point. The only problem is that that the 219°F reading is only accurate if the barometer is at 29.9 mm Hg. A thermometer needs to be recalibrated every time the barometric pressure rises or falls.

Syrup also needs to be packaged correctly to control bacterial growth in the container that can lead to spoilage. The syrup is packed into plastic jugs at 185°F. This prevents condensation, which can supply an environment for bacterial growth in the container. When bacterial colonies multiply within sap, they convert sucrose to glucose and other invert sugar molecules. This increase in invert sugar, when exposed to heat, will cause a darker product.

Your first competitor, Great North Maple, states on their bottle a clarity rating of Grade A with a brix (sugar) reading of 66.4 brix and a color of amber. You notice no crystallization of sugar in the bottle, which forecasts a low bacterial level of one colony per 10,000 milliliters.

Vermont Sweet Maple produces a tourist grade syrup with a clarity rating of Grade B, a brix reading of 68.3 brix, and a color of dark brown. The older samples have a higher-than-average bacterial count of one colony per 1,000 milliliters.

Ottawa Maple Syrup is a premium grade all-around syrup with a clarity rating of AA, a light amber color, and a sweetness reading of 67.1 brix.

You now measure West Geauga Maple Syrup to determine its clarity, color, and brix. The samples have a bacterial count as high as some commercial grades, and you note that there should be further research into either temperature at harvest time or cleanliness of equipment.

A table to compare these findings is useful.

[1] Atago website, https://www.agriculturesolutions.com/products/crop-soil-and-water-testing/refractometers-brix-meters/atago-pal-maple-digital-maple-syrup-refractometer-0-85-brix-detail, viewed February 23, 2016.
[2] Les Ober, Ohio Maple Blog, https://ohiomaple.wordpress.com/, Things You Can Do to Ensure the Quality of Your Maple Syrup, viewed February 23, 2016.
[3] Benjamin Cummings, "Bacterial Count in Colonies of Varying Solutions," Pearson Education, 2007.

Scenario 7
Comparison of the Fender Stratocaster and the Gibson Les Paul Guitars

You are an electrical engineer for a manufacturer of transducers, pickups, and microphones. The History Channel has decided to do a documentary special comparing two guitars that have shaped American music over the last 50 years—the Fender Stratocaster and the Gibson Les Paul.

Use the informal memorandum to report your findings to the program director of the History Channel. They are obviously looking for your expertise in the field of coils, yet they need other information such as:

1. Types of wood used in the body and neck
2. The tuning machine heads
3. Magnetic pickups
4. Volume controls
5. Tone controls

They are counting on you to report information in a nonbiased manner. Honesty is important.

They are expecting you to use several images and tables to display your findings. Any information you find must have documentation.

PEER REVIEW

Have another student review your work. Even though you may not be able to physically conduct the research in a real lab, through research you will be able to find enough data to convince the reader that your solution is the best.

VOCABULARY

grant
refractometer
simulate
subject matter expert (SME)

REFERENCES

Aeryon Labs Inc., http://www.aeryon.com/aeryon-skyranger, viewed September 29, 2016.

Minnesota Department of Transportation, "Unmanned Aerial Bridge Inspection Demonstration Report," Offices of Transportation Management, 1–24, 2016.

Matt Hayes, "Top 5 Reasons to Use a Drone for Bridge Inspection," http://rdoic.com/blog/top-5-reasons-to-use-a-drone-for-bridge-inspection#.V-0K1fArLIU, November 18, 2015, viewed September 29, 2016.

Rovdrone-Air and Water Industrial Inspections, http://rovdrone.eu/drone-en/industrial-inspections/bridge-inspections/, viewed September 29, 2016.

SenseFly by Albris, http://rdoic.com/products/uav/albris#.V_VyF-ArLIU, viewed October 2016.

Skycatch Evolution 3, http://www.suasnews.com/2015/12/40855/, viewed October 2016.

CHAPTER TEN

Writing a Proposal to Solve a Problem

Part 1: What's the Problem?

Estimated time to complete: 20–30 minutes

INTRODUCTION

In this chapter, you will write a winning proposal to acquire new business for your own company or one where you work. There are two main parts to this project. In this first part, you will decide on the topic of your proposal by recognizing a problem you would like to solve and then finding the best solution for one of the causes of the problem.

PROJECT OVERVIEW

How many times have you noticed something that could be improved with a simple solution? In your everyday routine you encounter all types of situations that make your life a little more difficult. By recognizing one of these problems you could possibly develop a solution to solve it. Being able to convince your reader that your idea is the most valid solution to their problem will ensure the acceptance of your idea. That idea is the first step of a proposal.

PROJECT DESIGN

The first part of this project will be creating a simple diagram that establishes the main problem you would like to solve in your proposal. When the drawing is finished, you will have successfully

SIDE BOX 10.1:
Companies Initiated at Home

Disney, the Wright Brothers, Amazon, Apple, Google, Mattel, Hewlett-Packard, Microsoft, Yankee Candle, Maglite, Harley Davidson, Lotus Cars, Dell

shown that you have recognized one of the causes of the problem and initiated a proposal that provides the best solution to that cause.

PROJECT DEVELOPMENT

The first thing you must do is to identify the *one problem* you would like to solve. The following exercise will give you some experience in devising a solution to a problem. Here is a list of common problems encountered by students across the country:[1]

- The cafeteria food is no good.
- Our Wi-Fi signal on campus is weak.
- The school's parking situation and the parking rates are crazy.
- There is too much stress.
- Mandatory prerequisites and electives add to the cost of school.

For this exercise you are to select the problem that affects you the most and turn it into an opportunity you can solve in your proposal.

- **Step 1.** Select one of the problems above and write it in the space below. This will be the focus of your proposal.

    The main problem you wish to solve:

    _____

_____

1 "College Complaints," online.udayton.edu, 2014.

- **Step 2.** Think about some of the possible causes of this problem and write them on the lines below:

  - Cause 1:

  - Cause 2:

  - Cause 3:

- **Step 3.** Now that you have identified several causes for the problem, select the one cause in Step 2 that you believe you are able to solve in your proposal. Write the cause you would like to solve in the space below:

  The cause of the main problem you will solve:

  _____

- **Step 4.** Write several solutions that can possibly solve the *cause* of your problem.

  - Solution 1:

  - Solution 2:

  - Solution 3:

- **Step 5.** Select the one *solution* you believe you can use to solve the *cause* (you have selected) to the main *problem*. Write it in the space below:

  Your solution to one of the causes of the main problem:

  _____

You are now ready to start Part 2. You will begin writing a proposal based on the exercise you have just completed. You will be given a new problem to solve yet the approach will be the same.

REMEMBER: The best proposals try to solve only *one* problem by addressing *one* of the causes with *one* solution.

PEER REVIEW

After you have selected your solution for this assignment, have a classmate review your work. They can give you an idea of how well your solution would work in a proposal.

Writing a Proposal to Solve a Problem

Part 2: A Proposal of Your Own

Estimated time to complete: 60–90 minutes

INTRODUCTION

In this chapter, you will write a winning proposal to acquire new business for your own company or where you work. This is the second part to this project. In this first part you decided on the topic of your proposal by recognizing a problem you would like to solve for your proposal and then finding the best solution for one of the causes of the problem. Now you will work on a unique problem and write a convincing proposal. It can be the same one you used in the first part of this section or a different one altogether.

PROJECT OVERVIEW

This proposal needs to be convincing, and therefore requires several sections that work together to present a convincing solution to the reader's problem. Each section is necessary and needs to be developed in a way that leads the reader to the conclusion that your proposal is the best solution to their dilemma.

PROJECT DESIGN

A well-written proposal contains all the information the buyer needs for your project to be accepted by them. Consider writing this proposal using the formal business letter format.

The heading of pages (after page 1) should include these three bits of information:

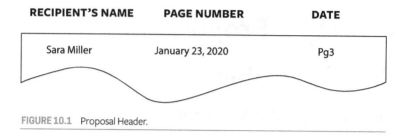

FIGURE 10.1 Proposal Header.

Note: You will use the name of the person receiving the proposal instead of your own.

This will help identify the pages in case some of them are lost or missing.

PROJECT DEVELOPMENT

- **Introduction:** The introduction should include these arguments, not necessarily in any specific order.[1]
  - State the subject and purpose of the proposal.
  - What is the background leading up to this solution?
  - Let the reader know the main problem your proposal will solve.
  - This should be an important solution for the reader's problem.
  - Give the reader a brief outline of the proposal.

- **Objective:** State the outcome of your proposal.
- **Scope of your services:** Explain exactly what you intend to provide as part of your services and products. Most important, disclose what services or products you will *not* provide.
- **Benefits and feasibility:** Let the reader understand the benefits of the proposal, how it has helped others in the past, and whether these results have been achieved before.

---

1 B. Yasin and H. Qamariah, "The Application of Swales' Model in Writing an Introduction to a Research Article," *Studies in English Language and Education (SIELE)* 1, no. 1 (2014): 31–44.

Also demonstrate significant improvements compared to the way things are at the present.

- **Qualifications/references:** It is important that the person reviewing this proposal understands that you are the best person to complete this project. Treat this section as if it were your resume. Show work experiences, any related projects, business references, and especially testimonials from previous customers.
- **Strategy:** What procedures did you put in place to achieve the clear goal of this proposal? Demonstrate the ways this proposal provides the best possible results.
- **Schedule:** Most businesses do not like to close their business or place their employees on leave while your work is being completed. Devise a schedule that is agreeable to their business hours.
- **Conclusions:** Make it obvious to the reader that this is your conclusion. Recap all the benefits you have stated earlier in the proposal and show the difference between how things are now, and how they will be with your solution in place. It is a good idea to show the total dollar amount of the project in your conclusion. If the reader understands everything the cost includes, it is not necessary to complete a cost schedule.
- **Optional cost schedule:** The cost schedule is included if there is a need to itemize the products and services used in the proposal. Itemizing will give the reader an opportunity to compare the value of your plan against the other proposals being considered by showing the products and services included in your scope.

REMEMBER: The best proposals try to solve only *one* problem by addressing *one* of the causes with *one* solution.

PEER REVIEW

After you have written your proposal for this assignment, have a classmate review your work. Your classmate will check to see that all the sections are properly developed and include the proper information.

VOCABULARY

internal/external
solicited/unsolicited
recipient
RFQ (or RFP)

CHAPTER ELEVEN

Working as a Team

Part 1: Developing Your Thesis Statement

Part 2: Researching Your Idea

Part 3: Paraphrasing the Written Word

Part 4: Developing an Oral Presentation

Part 5: Evaluating a Research Paper

INTRODUCTION

In this chapter, you and your partner will work together on five projects that are designed to assist you in writing a research paper. Your partner may be assigned to you or you may have selected someone with a common interest that you would like to research.

As you progress from one step to the next, you and your partner will understand the importance of teamwork. Cooperation is a key element in these projects, and you must be available to communicate your ideas with one another. Make sure you have each other's contact information before you begin.

Once you enter the workplace you will be judged partially on how capable you are in job-related knowledge. Most important, your employer is concerned with how well you work on a team of individuals with varied talents and personalities. How well will you get along with others in the workplace?

You will be graded on how well you and your partner evenly divided the workload and completed a paper on time following a specific design.

My partner's name:

_____

☐ I have my partner's contact information.

Working as a Team

Part 1: Developing Your Thesis Statement

Estimated time to complete: 20–30 minutes

INTRODUCTION

You and you partner will take the first step in writing a research paper. In this exercise, you will develop your thesis statement, which identifies the main argument or claim you wish to present to your reader.

PROJECT OVERVIEW

The thesis statement is simply a one-sentence explanation of the core of your paper so that it is obvious to the reader that you are taking a specific point of view. Your main argument should be narrow and fully explain the direction the paper will take. Define the scope of the research you will present to the reader; explain what you intend to cover and what you will not.

PROJECT DEVELOPMENT

Consider the following points as you move toward a final thesis statement.

1. What general topic is our team most interested in developing?

   _____

SIDE BOX 11.1.1:
Avoid an Ill-Defined Thesis Statement

Too general: Fire Drills at Work

Better: Developing Fire Drill Procedures for Your Office

Best: Insurance Company Requirements for Fire Escape Plans at Work Are Too Costly

2. Are we familiar with this topic from previous work or interests?

---

3. What would be the main point we would like to emphasize in our argument to the reader?

---

4. Can we cover the topic fully in the assigned space of the paper, or will the reader think that the paper is too short or too long?

---

5. Will we be able to present a neutral stance on this topic, or will we be inclined to present a biased argument based on passed perceptions of the topic?

---

6. Write your initial thesis statement in the space below:

---

7. Does the statement appear to be too general in its scope? If so, rewrite it with an emphasis on making it more clear-cut and concise.

PEER REVIEW

After you are satisfied with your thesis statement, have another group review your work. A good thesis statement should be controversial, narrow, and provide a basic ground plan for the entire paper that follows.

VOCABULARY

argument
controversial
narrow
scope
thesis

Working as a Team

Part 2: Researching Your Idea

Estimated time to complete: 20–30 minutes

INTRODUCTION

You and your partner will take the next step in writing a research paper. Together you will decide on the five or six main points you will present in your research paper and then research each of them by seeking related data in articles, books, websites, or any other legitimate sources of information.

PROJECT OVERVIEW

It is easier to break down your research into steps than to simply accumulate unrelated research sources that may or may not be connected. Your first task is to decide on the main structure of your paper and then to research each point you have constructed. You and your partner should divide the work evenly.

PROJECT DEVELOPMENT

In any order, write down the main points, or objectives, you would like to cover in your research paper. When writing your research objectives, focus on making sure the objectives are related to your thesis statement and what you are trying to achieve. Try to establish about five or six good sections that would cover the main argument you developed in the thesis statement and write them in the spaces marked "Topic."

NOTE: Do not include the Introduction or Conclusion as main topics.

SIDE BOX 11.2.1:
Worksheet Sample

THESIS STATEMENT: Early warning systems are not adequate for escaping the hazards of drilling for salt under Lake Erie.

1. Topic: Prefabricated tunnel sections are hazardous.
   a. Corporate catalog: Molnar Concrete Products, Inc., Mini-Catalog Edition, Chapter 1, 12–17, 2018.
   b. Website: "Defining Tube Tunnels," http://www.somesite.com/Tube Tunnels, viewed January 2, 2019.
   c. Jerold Chere, Patent
      · US 5678A, "Prefabricated Structures for Constructing Tunnels, Bridges and the Like," September 15, 1987.

THESIS STATEMENT:

1. Topic:

   a. Source:
   b. Source:
   c. Source:

2. Topic:

   a. Source:
   b. Source:
   c. Source:

3. Topic:

   a. Source:
   b. Source:
   c. Source:

4. Topic:

   a. Source:
   b. Source:
   c. Source:

5. Topic:

   a. Source:
   b. Source:
   c. Source:

After you are satisfied with the main topics of your paper, it is time to research each of the points individually. Try to find several unique sources for each of the sections by using your school library. You could visit the library in person or use an online database, depending on the resources available to you. The librarian can be a great aid in referring you to some ideas you may not have considered during your initial research.

The sources you cite should not all be websites. Search for books, journal articles, patents, websites, interviews, weblogs, or any legitimate source of information. List the sources individually after the word "Source" in the above form. Be sure you include all the information you can regarding each of the sources you intend to cite. There are several websites you can use to store this documentation for future use, as you would not want to lose any of your work to date.

DOCUMENTATION STYLES

You will need to select a method to document the sources you will cite in your research paper. These methods fall into two main categories, and each method has slight variations.

The first method is to place all your references into a bibliography and list them alphabetically by the author's last name. This is often referred to as "author–date" referencing or the Harvard System. When you refer to the source in the body of the paper, you use the author's last name and the date the material was published. This method is used by the Modern Language Association (MLA) and the American Psychological Association (APA).

The other common method is the numerical referencing or *endnote* system. In this system, the references are listed in the bibliography in the order that they appear in the paper and are identified with a number. Often the source is listed with the initials for the author's first name followed by the author's last name. In the body of your paper, you simply add a superscript number to identify the reference in the bibliography. This style is used in the Chicago Manual of Style (CMOS).

Be sure to comply with the method endorsed by your field of study. The Purdue Owl (Online Writing Lab) is an excellent website for details on the use of these citation/documentation methods.

PEER REVIEW

Another team should review your work up to this point to help you consider some alternate ideas for researching your main topics. By receiving input from others at this early stage, you can avoid mistakes and unnecessary efforts in your overall writing.

VOCABULARY

American Psychological Association (APA)
Chicago Manual of Style (CMOS)
Modern Language Association (MLA)
patent
weblog

Working as a Team

Part 3: Paraphrasing the Written Word

Estimated time to complete: 20–30 minutes

INTRODUCTION

Technical writing requires you to rewrite ideas and research from other scholarly sources. Even though you may be trying to rewrite the ideas of other authors into your own words, you still must give them credit for their original work. In this chapter you will understand the steps involved in paraphrasing one of the sources you will be using in your research paper.

PROJECT OVERVIEW

Writers need to be able to use other people's ideas and research to bolster their own writing. The use of credible research will make you more believable in the eyes of the reader.

Facts stand alone. You can state information from a dictionary or encyclopedia and the reader accepts this as fact. There is no need to cite or document facts.

The information you use in your thesis statement may be considered an opinion and needs to be supported by plausible research before the reader accepts your premise. This is the type of material that needs to be cited properly in your bibliography so that the reader can view the original sources of your arguments.

SIDE BOX 11.3.1:
Plagiarism Clarified

Paraphrasing is not switching just one word. Even though you are putting someone else's ideas into your own words, you must still give the author credit in your bibliography. Do not use direct passages from research without enclosing them in quotation marks. .

PROJECT DESIGN AND DEVELOPMENT

You and your partner should each select an article you would like to use in your research paper. Select it from the outline you created so that you can use it in your bibliography.

Use these steps in this paraphrasing assignment.

1. Select one of the sources you found for your research. Your partner should do the same. Start small with just a paragraph or two.

2. After you have read it over a few times, decide if the information is still appropriate to your thesis statement.

3. Write down any words you do not recognize and look them up in a dictionary or other source of reference. You may need to transfer these to a 3×5 card in the future for use in an oral presentation.

4. If you use any of these words in your paraphrase, you should enclose them in quotation marks. You may quote some text directly from your original source in quotation marks also. Do not do this unless the original text is so important that you should not try to paraphrase it; do not overdo it.

5. Review your version of what you wrote against the original text. Is it your own style? Make any adjustments as necessary.

6. Record the source in the citation style you decided to use at the bottom of your paraphrase. This way you can credit it easily if you decide to incorporate the material into your research paper.
7. Do not cut and paste information from your sources and use it as your own.
8. Use a plagiarism checker to make sure your work is yours and you can verify it.

PEER REVIEW

Partners can review each other's work in this exercise. Have your partner review the content from your research that you chose to paraphrase to see if you understood the article well enough to paraphrase. You should do the same for theirs.

VOCABULARY

paraphrase
plagiarism
plausible

Working as a Team

Part 4: Developing an Oral Presentation

Estimated time to complete: 20–30 minutes

INTRODUCTION

In this chapter, you will decide on the type of media you will use to present the main objective of your research paper to an audience. Several types of presentation software are available, with PowerPoint being the most common. However, you may decide that another means is more to your style.

PROJECT OVERVIEW

There is an art to developing PowerPoint slides, posters, or hand-outs for your presentation that support your research paper. This is a good time to start thinking about the medium you and your partner will select for this project. Now that you have an outline of the paper you are writing, it will be easier to begin the first step.

PROJECT DESIGN

Preparing the Presentation

- Use the outline of your research paper. This outline serves another purpose because it provides you headings for all your slides in the order you wish to present them.
- Clarify jargon and technical terms. Your audience may not understand certain terminology that is common to your profession.

SIDE BOX 11.4.1:
The Best Slides

If you are using PowerPoint for your presentation, limit the text on your slides as if you were creating a billboard that is fast and easy to read while capturing the main idea of your presentation at that moment.

- Know your key points and repeat them often. It is not uncommon to repeat your message three or four times to stress its importance.
- Test for length of time. The venue where you are speaking should give you a time slot for your presentation. Do not be too short or too long, as other speakers will be scheduled.
- Make 3 × 5 note cards. These are not as distracting as holding up large 8 1/2 × 11 sheets of paper. They are also useful in helping you remember long names or technical information critical to your speech.
- Use supporting graphics. The image on your slide should clearly support the idea you are talking about for the duration of that slide.
- Print handouts. These are optional, but are helpful in assisting the audience in following your talk.
- Posters may be required. Some locales require that you have a poster available to attract like-minded people to your presentation.
- Dress appropriately.

Check Your Slides

- Do not use dark text over a dark background or light text against a light background.
- Do not use text that is too small to read.
- Use templates if you are unable to create your own designs.
- Do not use too much text on one slide.
- Make sure you have enough slides.

Three Types of Slides

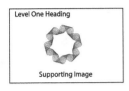

Level One Heading	Level One Heading	Level One Heading
Supporting Image	• Bullet point • Bullet Point • Bullet point	Lorem ipsum dolor sit amet, consectetuer adipiscing elit, sed diam nonummy nibh euismod tincidunt ut laoreet dolore magna aliquam erat volutpat. Ut wisi enim ad minim veniam, quis nostrud. Lorem ipsum dolor sit amet, consectetuer adipiscing elit, sed do eiusmod tempor incididunt ut labore et dolore magna aliqua. Ut enim ad minim veniam, quis nostrud exercitation ullamco laboris nisi ut aliquip ex ea commodo consequat.

FIGURE 11.4.1   Three Types Slides.

PRESENTATION   BULLET LIST   TEXT

- Presentation (sentence with image). This slide is often considered your best choice as the listener will look at the main sentence and view the image very rapidly. Now you have their attention, and listening to you becomes the focus.
- Bullet list (technical data). This is an effective slide to help you remember the key points you wish to discuss at this point in your presentation. If the slide contains only the main points you intend to discuss, the spotlight will still be on you as the focal point. It is also a great way to define technical terms that the listeners may not understand.
- Text slide (try to avoid). Slides with too much text convey another message: you do not know your topic. You will not be able to read the slides faster than your audience, and they will find other things to do rather than listening to your talk. This is also a sign of being unprepared.

PROJECT DEVELOPMENT

In Chapter 11.2 you and your partner decided on the main sections you would develop in your research paper. Then you decided on the second- and third-level headings that could be used to finish the outline of your research paper.

For this project you can use all the headings you developed in the Chapter 11.2 outline and develop presentation slides, posters, or handouts to enhance your speech. Keep in mind that the best slides do not distract the listeners from what you have to say. They should not contain too much text; one descriptive sentence works best.

PEER REVIEW

Have another team review your slides to verify the following:

- Do the slides convey the main idea of the topic you are discussing?
- Are there enough slides?
- Can the fonts be read from a distance?

VOCABULARY

billboard
jargon
terminology
venue

Working as a Team

Part 5: Evaluating a Research Paper

Estimated time to complete: 20–30 minutes

INTRODUCTION

In this chapter you will review a research paper written by another student. Find a paper from a previous semester to use for this exercise. This lesson will aid in understanding common mistakes made by others that you can avoid in your paper. It will also demonstrate some of the strengths of other students in following the proper structure of the research paper.

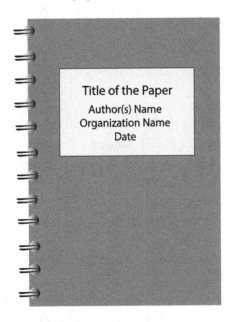

Title of the Paper
Author(s) Name
Organization Name
Date

FIGURE 11.5.1   Packaging a Report.

PROJECT OVERVIEW

Sometimes it is easier to view a completed version of a project you are about to begin. Not only will you view a completed research paper, but you will be given the opportunity to discuss its strengths and weaknesses. Once you are familiar with the sections used in a typical research paper you can begin this assignment.

PROJECT DESIGN

Follow the guidelines to recognize the type of content to be developed in each section of a typical research paper. Once you understand how the paper unfolds you will be able to correct each section based on the criteria listed below.

Front Matter

The first five sections are referred to as the front matter because they serve as a preface or introduction to the research paper. They act as a roadmap for the reader to designate the sections and content of the paper.

1. Letter of Transmittal. This formal letter is attached to the outside of the report and designates the intended purpose of the document.
2. Cover and label. The cover should be sturdy and not fall apart once the report is opened. The label shows the title of the paper, the author(s), name of the organization or business, and the date.
3. Executive Summary (Abstract). This is a summary of the report for the purpose of informing the reader of a summary of the document.
4. Dedication. If so desired, add this page to acknowledge an individual or group for special assistance with the report.
5. Table of Contents. This can be automatically generated in Office by using the command under the References tab called Table of Contents. Word will then generate the table along with the logical order of headings and a page

number. If you change your paper by adding or deleting pages, there is also an Update Table command in the same area.

6. List of Figures. There is another tab under References called Insert Table of Figures. Word then searches your document for the captions style and uses those to create or update this section.

Main Body

This section is the actual report. It should be organized so that the reader is able to easily recognize the major headings and the subheadings listed under them. All headings should be labeled with the same text as found in the Table of Contents. This is automatically achieved in Microsoft Office if you use the *styles* designed for the document. All images should be labeled under the picture, using the same name found in the List of Figures.

1. Introduction. Tell them what you are going to tell them.
2. Body of report. Tell them.
3. Conclusion. Tell them what you just told them.

Back Matter

1. Bibliography. This section should list all the citations used in the paper according to the method used by the author(s). Once a style is used it should be applied consistently throughout the whole paper (MLA, CMOS, or APA).

SIDE BOX 11.5.1:
Page Numbering

All pages in the front matter use lowercase Roman numerals to number the pages (i, ii, iii, iv, and so on). The Letter of Transmittal is not included in the numbering.

The main body uses Arabic, or cardinal, numbers, starting with the Introduction (1, 2, 3, 4, and so on). Even though the Introduction is included in the numbering process, you do not see the page number on the actual page. This is often true for the first pages of chapters and other major sections.

2. Appendix. This section may be used for large foldout pages that can be referred to throughout the main body of the paper. It could also include a glossary or other sections to clarify meanings of jargon or symbols unfamiliar to the reader.

PROJECT DEVELOPMENT

This section contains an outline to assist you in reviewing or grading a typical research paper. A guide to grading a document is often called a rubric. It is important that each section in the research paper is in the proper order and contains appropriate information for that section.

As you grade the paper try and use a system that allows you to assign a greater penalty for major mistakes. For example, a misspelled word would not be as great a mistake as a completely missing section.

Letter of Transmittal

- Topic is in italics.
- Purpose is clearly stated.
- Acknowledgments are provided.
- Gesture of goodwill/ contact information is included.
- Formal business letter format is used.

Report Cover

- Solid.
- Includes title, names, organization, date.

Abstract/Executive Summary

Table of Contents

- Organized into clear sections.
- Consistent with headings inside paper.
- Vertical alignment is correctly applied.

List of Figures and Tables

- Same design used as TOC.
- Separates tables from images.
- Same names appear under images.

Grammar, Punctuation, Spelling

Introduction

- States the purpose of the paper.
- Identifies the intended audience.
- States the need for the paper.

Body

- Correct spacing between lines.
- Consistent use of fonts.
- All images and tables labeled properly.
- Headings are clearly marked.
- References are either numbered in the order of appearance or alphabetical by author's last name.
- Bibliography should not be all websites.

Conclusion

- States the final argument based on the material presented to the reader.

Page Numbering

- Front matter all lower-case Roman numerals.
- Introduction begins with Arabic numeral 1, but the number is not visible on the page itself.

PEER REVIEW

After you have graded a research paper have another student or team review your criticism of the paper. Hopefully you will have a better understanding of the expectations of your reader as they review a scholarly document.

VOCABULARY

glossary
jargon
Letter of Transmittal
Preface
Table of Contents

CHAPTER TWELVE

Using Robert's Rules of Order

Estimated time to complete: 20–30 minutes

INTRODUCTION

Parliamentary procedure has been used in meetings since the seventeenth century. It is a civilized method of maintaining order among all the participants of group sessions and ensures each member a chance to be heard, regardless of the size of the group. One of the most common methods for running a meeting is *Robert's Rules of Order* (1876) written by Henry Martyn Robert.

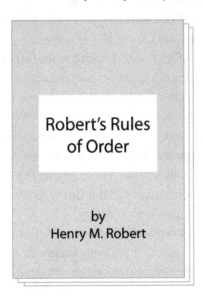

Robert's Rules
of Order

by
Henry M. Robert

FIGURE 12.1   Roberts Rules of Order.

PROJECT OVERVIEW

In this class, you will participate in an actual meeting using *Robert's Rules of Order* so that you can experience all the sections of a meeting and the procedures involved in conducting one's self in the group. One person is randomly selected to chair (or head) the meeting and that person will be able to follow a script in the *Project Development* section to assist them in running the meeting.

PROJECT DESIGN

When using parliamentary procedure as presented in *Robert's Rules of Order*, the meeting generally has 10 distinct sections:

1. **Call to order.** The meeting begins promptly at the designated time with a call to order by the meeting chair. If the chair is not present at the start of the meeting, anyone may call the meeting to order.

2. **Roll call.** The recording secretary will note the names of all those attending the meeting.

3. **Reading of the minutes.** The recording secretary then reads the notes from the last meeting to inform the attendees of what was recorded at the last meeting. This is a way of reminding those in attendance of what occurred the last meeting. These minutes must be approved by those in attendance before the meeting continues. There may be a need to correct, delete, or add information.

4. **Officer reports.** Reports from other elected officials can be given at this point. For example, the treasurer could inform the group of expenditures, income, and balances in the organization's treasury.

5. **Committee reports.** Most committees are members who have volunteered to perform necessary tasks within the group. Some committees may be ongoing, such as a membership committee or a special events committee. Some committees are formed to temporarily report on a specific subject or purpose and then disbanded after their final

report. These are called "ad hoc" committees (Latin for "to this").

6. **Special orders.** Important business previously designated for consideration at this meeting.

7. **Unfinished business.** There may not have been enough time designated for the last meeting and because of the lack of time the discussion on certain matters has been moved to this meeting.

8. **New business.** This is the section of the meeting where members can present new ideas to the group using a motion. If it is a good idea or recommendation, another member may second the motion, allowing others to discuss and eventually vote on the idea.

9. **Announcements.** The chair or recording secretary should remind members of upcoming events or other information such as the time and date of the next meeting.

10. **Adjournment.** A motion is made to end the meeting. A second motion is required. A majority vote is then required for the meeting to be adjourned.

SIDE BOX 12.1:
Recording Secretary's Duty

In addition to taking attendance, the recording secretary should take complete notes on all that is discussed at the meeting. All votes and their outcomes are recorded. This person should also conduct correspondence among all the members and keep all records and files.

Defining Motions

A motion is a proposal that the entire membership can act on and is a way all members can express themselves.

How to Present a Motion

1. Obtain the floor.
   - Wait until the last speaker has finished.
   - Stand (or raise hand) and address the chair by saying, "Mr./Ms. Chair."
   - Wait until the chair recognizes you.
2. Make your motion.
3. Speak in a clear and concise manner.
4. Always state a motion affirmatively. Say, "I move that we ...," rather than "I move that we do not ..." (if you state the motion in a negative manner it is confusing to the assembly when the time comes to vote on the motion).
5. Avoid personalities and stay on your subject.
6. Wait for someone to second your motion.
7. Another member will second your motion or the chair will call for a second.
8. If there is no second to your motion, it is lost.
9. You may need more information. Say, "Point of information," and ask your question.
10. The chair restates your motion.
11. The chair will say, "It has been moved and seconded that we ...," thus placing your motion before the membership for consideration and action.
12. It now belongs to the assembly. The membership then either debates your motion or moves directly to a vote.

Any member may:

- Call the meeting to order.
- Second motions.
- Debate motions.
- Vote on motions.

Voting on a Motion

- By voice. Members can vote by declaring their vote aloud.
- By roll call. Each member is asked to cast a vote after their name is called. This is often used in government as each individual signs their name in a ledger and casts their vote one by one.
- By general consent. This is very common in small groups where it is easier to ask all those in favor to say "Aye."
- By division. This is a method for taking a better estimate of a vote than a voice vote. Typically, a division is taken when the result of a voice vote is challenged or when a two-thirds vote is required.
- By ballot. This type of vote is used for members to declare their vote in a private manner. It can be done by writing the vote on a piece of paper.

The chair puts the motion to the assembly for vote.

"Those in favor of adopting the motion to _____ say 'Aye.' [pause] Those opposed say 'No.'"

After the vote has been taken, it is the role of the chair to announce the results of the vote to the assembly. The chair could say:

"The (ayes or noes) have it."

The following script can be used by the group's chairperson to guide everyone along through their first meeting. The topic of the meeting should be assigned before the meeting so that each participant can prepare something to contribute to the session.

The topic can be a short article to read or a discussion of an upcoming event for the group. Be sure that you have prepared so that you can be a part of the discussion.

Possible topics:

- Fundraising
- Classroom competitions
- Proper conduct in the workplace
- Importance of preparation

PROJECT DEVELOPMENT

Meeting Agenda

TOPIC: "What does it take to develop a successful career?"
A. Call to Order
Leader: "I will now call our first meeting to order. First I need a volunteer to take the minutes of this meeting."
<IF NO VOLUNTEER, APPOINT THE PERSON ON YOUR LEFT.>

B. Roll Call
Leader: "At this time, the secretary will take attendance."
Secretary: <Secretary calls all names>

C. Read Minutes
Leader: "As this is the first meeting there are no minutes from a last meeting. You should all have a copy of the discussion points for this meeting on your desk."
Leader: "Are there are any corrections or additions to today's agenda?"
"I motion to approve today's agenda and proceed."
<SOMEONE MUST SECOND THE MOTION>
Leader: "All in favor say 'Aye,' opposed. ..."
Secretary: <record the vote>

D. Today's Agenda
Leader: "Today you are reporting to me on 'What does it take to develop a successful career?'"
<ASK FOR VOLUNTEERS TO BEGIN DISCUSSION>
<The secretary should take notes on the discussion. They do not have to be word for word, but a good summary of the ideas presented to the group by each member.>

E. New Business

Leader: "Is there any new business or special offers?"
<AT THIS POINT ANY MEMBER MAY PRESENT AN IDEA TO THE GROUP TO DISCUSS AND VOTE ON FOR FUTURE IMPLEMENTATION.>

STEP	WHAT TO SAY
1. The member rises and addresses the chair.	"Mr./Madam Chair."
2. The chair recognizes the member.	"The chair recognizes Mr./Ms. _____."
3. The member makes a motion.	"I move to _____."
4. Another member must second the motion.	"Second."
5. The chair states the motion.	Point of information may be asked to clarify the motion.
6. The members debate the motion.	"It is moved and seconded to _____."
7. Are we ready to vote?	"Let us discuss this issue."
8. The chair puts the question, and the members vote.	"Those in favor of adopting the motion to _____ say 'Aye.' [pause]. Those opposed say 'No.'"
9. The chair announces the result of the vote. The vote is recorded by the secretary.	"The (ayes or noes) have it."

F. SUMMARY OF DECISIONS MADE (for next meeting's minutes)
<ONCE THE DISCUSSIONS ARE ENDED THE SECRETARY CAN READ THE MINUTES OF TODAY'S MEETING.>
Secretary: "As a group we have come to the following conclusions: <READ TODAY'S NOTES>."

G. ANNOUNCEMENTS

H. Motion to Adjourn (someone must second this motion)
Leader: "If there is no new business I would like to motion to adjourn."
Leader: <IF SOMEONE SECONDS THE MOTION TAKE A VOTE TO ADJOURN.>
Leader: "This meeting is adjourned."

PEER REVIEW

Once the meeting has successfully concluded, each member should have a better understanding of how to conduct themselves at a meeting. The moderator can offer a critique of each member's performance, the chair's role in guiding the meeting, and the efficiency of the recording secretary in note taking.

VOCABULARY

adjourn
minutes
parliamentary procedure
point of information

CHAPTER THIRTEEN

Voicing Your Podcast

Estimated time to complete: 20–30 minutes

INTRODUCTION

Online videos comprise a large portion of social media, providing both entertainment and instructional material. For this project you will decide on a topic that you are interested in developing into either a video or sound file. You will then upload the file to a web server where it can be viewed or heard later by any other individual with an interest in your topic or a need for the information you are providing as a subject matter expert (SME). You can use videos to review a product, repair it, or compare it to similar merchandise.

PROJECT OVERVIEW

The first thing you will decide is if you wish to record only your voice (podcast) or develop a video with both video and sound (vodcast or videocast). If you think your audience is just interested in what you have to say, then a podcast would be a good choice. Podcasts generally contain political content, sports analysis, or even music. They can be listened to at the user's convenience.

The vodcast would be beneficial if there is a need to show how to perform a certain task that requires visual input. Typically, vodcasts show car or appliance repair, music lessons, computer software explanations, and so on. This gives the viewer a chance to follow at their own pace while pausing and restarting the video.

PROJECT DESIGN

A podcast is a digital media file, or a series of such files, that is distributed over the internet using syndication feeds for

SIDE BOX 13.1:
Recording Podcasts

Many online tools are available for recording your podcast or vodcast for this assignment. Audacity, Zencastr, and Auphonic are open source software for voice recording and editing. There are even smartphone apps, such as Anchor and AntennaPod. Both Windows and Mac ship with recording software and an internal microphone.

SIDE BOX 13.2:
Recording Vodcasts

For recording video content, you can try websites like ScreenCast-O-Matic or screen-capturing software like CamStudio. Your smartphone also has capability to record and upload your video.

playback on portable media players and personal computers. Typical formats are MP3, WAV, WMA, and AIFF, depending on your operating system.

A vodcast, or video podcast, contains both video and audio and is the most difficult to create and view. A vodcast can be created using a digital camcorder and video editing software such as iMovie or Movie Maker. Typical formats are MP4 and *MOV*.

Podcasts and vodcasts share the following features:

- Can be a one-time production.
- Often a serial production where new "episodes" are produced daily, weekly, or monthly.
- Download automatically when the author or "podcaster" uploads new content.
- Listened to whenever and wherever the user has time. Listeners can be notified of new episodes via email.

PROJECT DEVELOPMENT

Follow these basic steps in recording your first podcast or vodcast:

1. **Come up with an idea.** Select a topic you enjoy talking about. This will give you an advantage when it comes time to develop your topic.
2. **Write a script.** You may want to write down an outline of the main points you wish to discuss. It is easy to remove any unwanted sections in the final file by selecting and deleting them.

3. **Consider length.** Too long of a recording will result in a large file that may take too long to download. Also, viewers may find it more interesting to view smaller segments that are several minutes long, similar to episodes.

4. **Record the sound and video.** Use the external or built-in microphone/camera on the computer or smartphone or select a website that allows you to do so.

5. **Save the file in the desired format.** This may depend on your operating system. Try and select a compressed format such as MP3 or MP4 to reduce the file size. Even though these files have been modified, the final product should still sound first rate.

6. **Add finishing touches.** Transitions, text overlays, or graphics will add a professional touch to your finished project and will enhance your credibility with the audience.

7. **Publish (or upload) your file.** Several online sites such as Vimeo, YouTube, or DailyMotion will welcome your project.

There are many free, open-source audio recorders and editors that you can use with Windows, Mac, or Linux. They often install with the LAME MP3 encoder that allows you to export your file to MP3 format.

You will need:

- An internal microphone or a microphone plugged into your computer's microphone-in jack or USB port.
- A set of headphones to prevent feedback as you record your message.
- A server on which to post or upload the finished file.

Most sound recording programs have similar interfaces based on universal symbols.

1. Adjust the recording volume by dragging the slider near the microphone icon.

2. Click the red button (identified by a circle) to begin recording. An audio track will appear.

3. Click the yellow button to pause recording.

4. Click the green button to play back the recording.

5. To select a portion of the audio track, click the selection tool.
6. Click and drag across the desired area to cut, copy, or delete.
7. Choose "File > Export as MP3" from the menu bar. The "Save MP3 File As" dialog box will open, and you can fill in your name and title.

If you do not have the "LAME" plugin installed, you may get an error. Some versions of recording software come with this encoder already enclosed.

PEER REVIEW

Once your podcast is published send a link to your classmates. Ask them to give it a thumbs up or thumbs down. This will give you an indication of how well it is received by your viewers. You may also develop a following based on the popularity of your content, and this is the best way of knowing your work is a success.

VOCABULARY

bit rate
compressed
LAME
open source
transitions

CHAPTER FOURTEEN

Publishing Your Own Weblog

Estimated time to complete: 20–30 minutes

INTRODUCTION

Many writers are using the internet to publish their ideas in a format that is easy to access and even easier to create. The weblog (or blog) is a great way to keep an online diary of your current work and thoughts on any number of topics. In this chapter, you will set up and write your original thoughts for anyone to view.

PROJECT OVERVIEW

Once you decide on the purpose of your blog you can begin the design process. Selecting fonts and artwork should reflect the content of your blog. Is it serious or humorous? Does it relate a specific topic such as sports, cooking recipes, or political comment?

You may start on one or more articles at a time and keep them in a separate section of the hosting site until they are ready for viewing by the public. This way nothing is viewed until you consider it finished.

PROJECT DESIGN

A blog (or weblog) is your own website that you can use to publish your ideas, opinions, or just a daily diary of events in your life. Once you decide on a format that best fits your writing style, you can start on the basic look of the site that you are developing. You will find that the hosting sites offer quite a few templates you can use to give your work a professional look. Some of these sites offer an indexing feature that allows you to keep track of all your

SIDE BOX 14.1:
Create Your Blog

There are many online sites available for you to develop a blog, and many of them are free to use, such as Word-Press, Wix, SiteBuilder, Blogger, Tumbler, and many more. Research a few of them to see which ones offer the development tools and features that match your needs.

individual essays in a table of contents. There are even counters to keep track of the number of visitors to your blog.

Visitors to your site should be given the opportunity to subscribe to your blog so that can be informed every time you publish a new article. Your visitors can also have a section where they can post feedback to your articles.

PROJECT DEVELOPMENT

1. The first thing you need to do is create a memorable name for your blog. You should come up with one that is easy to remember and reflects the content of your work.

2. Pick a hosting site for your blog. Check online for a review of the site to see how well they provide services such as customer support and see if they are free or require a monthly fee. Those that require a monthly fee may provide special services that you would require, especially if you decide to charge viewers to access your blog.

3. The hosting site will give you a URL so that others will be able to access your blog. It is usually the name of the site followed by your blog's name, such as: www. bloghost.com/*myBlogName*.

4. Select a design or theme for your site. Most are free of charge, and there are quite a few available at an extra cost to really give your blog a professional appearance. It

is also a nice touch to develop your own logo to place on the top of the page.

5. Gather any images, charts, or graphs that you would like to use in your blog and make sure they are of decent quality and resolution.

6. Pick the topic of your first blog and begin writing. Once you feel it is refined enough to view, publish it to the main page of your site.

PEER REVIEW

Visitors to your blog should have a space where they can give you instant feedback to the articles you are writing. Take all criticism as being constructive and use it to improve the navigation, content, and appearance of your blog.

VOCABULARY

logo
template
URL

CHAPTER FIFTEEN

Creating a Poster for Presentations

Estimated time to complete: 40–50 minutes

INTRODUCTION

Why are posters used? Very often someone passing by your booth in a tradeshow will see your poster and be attracted to the topic of your presentation. Posters assist in attracting members of the same field of study and do so without any preliminary conversation. Very often people feel harassed and would rather investigate on their own instead of being constantly annoyed by booth attendants. Another good use of posters is to clarify your presentation by summarizing the major distinct sections of your speech within framed sections. You will be able to create a well-designed poster in this lesson that can serve either purpose.

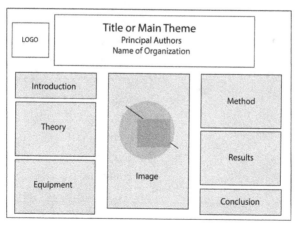

FIGURE 15.1   Poster Example.

PROJECT OVERVIEW

You can use just about any popular drawing tool to create a basic poster illustrating the research you and your partner may have completed in previous assignments. You will select the size of the poster, color palette, what sections to include, images, and whether it should be portrait or landscape in design. This exercise uses PowerPoint as the main drawing tool. You may select any other that allows you to export to a large image format.

PROJECT DESIGN

Keep the following in mind when designing your poster:

1. The poster must be aesthetically pleasing to attract viewers.
2. It must communicate clearly and concisely the essential points of the study. You want others to be able to replicate your research and get the same results that you did.
3. Landscape format is most common. Check with conference organizer on specific details.
4. Common poster sizes are 24 × 36, 42 × 32, 48 × 27, 48 × 36, and 54 × 34 inches.
5. Most posters have three or four columns.
6. Portrait or landscape orientation can be used depending on your tastes or requirements.

7. Pastel or white backgrounds will allow the text on your poster to stand out better.
8. Frame all the sections in little boxes so that each element is recognizable and easy to find when scanning the poster.

PROJECT DEVELOPMENT

Making Posters in PowerPoint

- Online templates are available with printing and mounting.
- You can make your own custom posters in PowerPoint.
  - Go to Design > Slide Size
  - Design > Theme for templates
  - Design > Variant (colors) to change the color scheme to fit your organization's colors or logo.

- Use the Grids and Guides feature to show grid lines that will assist you in the alignment of text and graphics. These lines will not print on the final poster. Right-click anywhere on the screen. Select "Grids and Guides," and then select "Display drawing guides on screen."

FIGURE 15.2   Drawing Guides.

Posters at Professional Society Meetings

- Readers should be able to view the main ideas of your poster from 10 feet away.
- They should also understand the meaning of your research within one minute.
- Encourage discussion from other attendees.

Typical Sections on a Poster

- **Title section.** Include your logo, names of all principal investigators (PIs), and the name of the organization.
- **Abstract.** As always, this section relates a short version of your research to attract like-minded people.
- **Introduction.** If you need the space, combine this with the Abstract section.
- **Equipment, methods, and procedures.** List important items necessary to complete the research in a consistent manner.
- **Results of your research.** Were the results what you expected, or did you arrive at different outcomes?
- **Discussion or conclusions.** Be sure to use your research to come to proper conclusions.
- **Implications for further research.** Do not close your research at this stage. There could be more investigative work to continue your investigation.
- **References.** You can briefly list these on the poster. It may be better to have them detailed on a handout.
- **Acknowledgments.** Recognize help from other sources.

How to Remove the Image Background (Bounding Box)

Most images do not have a transparent background; that is, one that allows you to see the text or other images that are layered behind it. PowerPoint and other graphic programs have tools to remove parts of the background so that the image is considered "transparent," allowing you to see other information in your presentation. For convenience, this example uses PowerPoint.

- Place or import your image into the drawing area.
- Select it with the mouse pointer.
- Go to the tab at the top ribbon marked "Picture tools."

- Select the icon "Remove background," which is usually on the left side of the top ribbon.

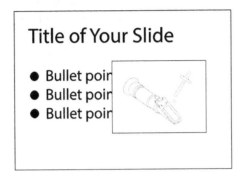

FIGURE 15.3   (a) Image background hides other information (b) Slide Image.

- You will notice that all the parts of the background that can be removed are identified with a purplish color called magenta.
- Before you finalize your edit, you may select or deselect additional portions of the image with the selection tool.
- Once you are satisfied with the parts you wish to remove, click "Keep Changes."
- You will now have an image with the transparent sections you defined.

Title of Your Slide

- Bullet point one
- Bullet point two
- Bullet point three

FIGURE 15.4   Results of background removal.

Production

- In PowerPoint, save the file using "Save as Adobe PDF Portable Document Format (PDF)" or "Export as Adobe PDF."

- Using the PDF file, the poster can be printed on a wide-format printer and then glued to a backing board to give it strength and to help it stand properly without collapsing.
- If you are presenting in another city, try to have the printing and other production done at the remote location to eliminate damage to the poster. Some companies will even deliver the poster to the site of your presentation.

Poster Presentation Tactics

- Dress for the occasion.
- Do not wear distracting jewelry, hats, or loud clothing.
- Keep your hands out of your pockets.
- Do not block the view of your poster.
- Do not harass other attendees as they pass by.
- Prepare handouts to help others remember your work.
- A product specification sheet could be useful.

PEER REVIEW

Have classmates walk by your poster to see if it meets the requirements listed in the above sections. The poster should be artistically balanced, viewable from 10 feet, and the main idea should be understood in less than a minute.

VOCABULARY

backerboard
bounding box
grid
PDF
replicate

CHAPTER SIXTEEN

Rethinking the Researcher's Notebook

Estimated time to complete: 20–30 minutes

INTRODUCTION

Before the advent of computers, smartphones, and tablets, most engineers and scientists kept a small notebook to keep track of ideas they were developing into more important works of research. The notebook was usually small enough to carry in a pocket or briefcase and was available at a moment's notice to jot down a blossoming idea no matter where or when it happened. In this chapter, we will take a better look at this method of recording one's thoughts and some of the ways you can record drawings and other data.

FIGURE 16.1   The Researcher's Notebook.

PROJECT OVERVIEW

First, you will review the types of information that are usually recorded in this notebook. The notebook can include handwritten notes, formulas, and images depicting prototype designs. Such

SIDE BOX 16.1:
Keeping the Embargo

If you are ever asked to witness or review a document marked "proprietary," you must remember that you are not allowed to divulge any of the information you are witnessing in that document until it has been made public through either the printed or spoken word. This is also called "keeping the embargo"—a pledge of secrecy.

images can be either three-dimensional (isometric) or two-dimensional figures (orthogonal) on the graph paper. Pictures of items can be taped onto the pages to help illustrate an idea.

As you look at Figure 16.2, notice that the angle in the drawing is at 30 degrees and all other lines are perfectly horizontal or vertical.

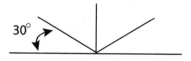

FIGURE 16.2   An Isometric Drawing.

FIGURE 16.3   An Orthogonal Drawing.

In Figure 16.3, it is necessary to show a side view and an end view of the pipe to clearly indicate that it has an inner diameter that is circular. With one of the drawings missing it is very difficult to determine if the drawing is a rectangle or a ring.

PROJECT DESIGN

One of the main components of the researcher's notebook is hand-drawn illustrations. Drawing figures is a skill worth learning. With today's 3D-printing processes, it is vital to represent drawings illustrating the depth, length, and width of an object before it can be successfully created. In this exercise, you learn to represent objects in both three-dimensional and two-dimensional representation.

PROJECT DEVELOPMENT

This object is an isometric rendition of a three-dimensional object.

1. Draw the object in the space below, shading the object in a way to depict light showing on the different sides.
2. Redraw the same object as it would appear in a 90-degree, clockwise rotation; keep the light originating from the same point. Keep in mind that all angled lines are represented at 30 degrees and are parallel to each other.
3. The graph paper in Figure 16.5 is designed to assist you in drawing the lines at the correct angles.

This type of drawing does not have a vanishing point. In other words, objects do not appear to become smaller at the back than the front. They stay the same size, giving them a somewhat distorted look.

An important point to remember is that in isometric drawings all angled lines are parallel at 30 degrees and all vertical lines are also parallel. The three-dimensional look is enhanced by employing a light source shining down on your object. The sides of the drawing that get full light will be lighter than the sides receiving little or no light.

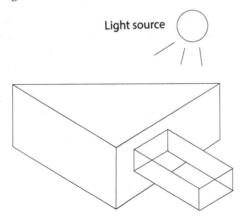

FIGURE 16.4   Redrawing a 3D Isometric Shape.

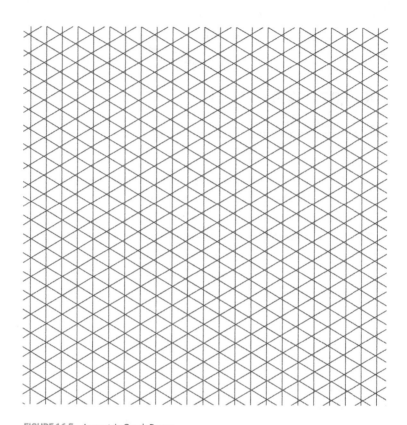

FIGURE 16.5 Isometric Graph Paper.

PEER REVIEW

Allow another student to judge your drawing to see how well you depicted the object. There should be evidence of light shining down on the drawing to help show the quality of a three-dimensional figure. Are the 30-degree angled lines parallel? Are other lines parallel to the horizon? Are the objects in scale to one another?

With the light in a stationary position, do the objects receive different levels of shading as they are turned from one drawing to the next?

VOCABULARY

isometric
orthogonal
proprietary
vanishing point

CHAPTER SEVENTEEN

Translating International Communications

Estimated time to complete: 20–30 minutes

INTRODUCTION

As businesses and schools rely more and more on communicating with other cultures, it becomes important to know how to assemble your documents so that they are translated in an appropriate manner.

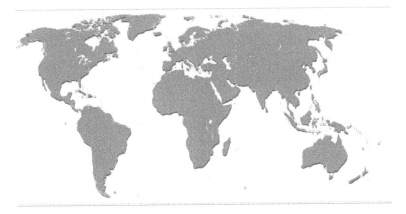

FIGURE 17.1   Blank Map-World.

PROJECT OVERVIEW

This chapter is designed to help you understand the most appropriate ways to translate documents from one language to another. You will select a city from a list of international locations and discover information important to a good translation. Then you will discover some of the points of local interest and everyday facts important to the people who live in that city.

Using this information, you should be able to write an email request to a citizen of that city using inappropriate language following the customs of the recipient.

PROJECT DESIGN

There are different stages of translating from one language to another.

Word-for-word. Direct conversion of text from one language to another based on a literal translation of your language.

Document assembly. Preparing information in your writing so that it translates properly on many different levels.

Regional analysis. Not just translating text to another language, but optimizing the information for the specific target culture by:

- Considering local standards.
- Converting currencies for accurate pricing.
- Applying regional symbols and signs.
- Adjusting visuals to remove potentially offensive elements.
- Accommodating regional formats, such as paper size.
- Using culturally relevant examples and images when possible.
- Using international symbols and formats for items like date, time, or drawings.

Preparing a Manuscript for Translation

- Do not omit direct or indirect articles.
  Before: Reports will be placed in mailboxes.
  After: **The** reports will be placed in **the** mailboxes.

- Repeat nouns rather than using pronouns.
  Unclear: There are three nurses and three interpreters on duty. **They** speak Croatian, Serbian, Greek, and Italian.
  Clear: There are three nurses and three interpreters on duty. **The three nurses and three interpreters** speak Croatian, Serbian, Greek, and Italian.

- Avoid fancy words; speak in the language of the common man.
  For example: Replace the word "preposterous" with "silly" and the word "corroborated" with "verify."

- Avoid metaphors, colloquialisms, and culturally specific humor. These are usually untranslatable.
  For example: I am so hungry I could eat a horse.
  My car can stop on a dime.

- Include both Standard and International Measurements.
  For example: The container holds 1 gallon (3.8 liters).

Translation Services

- Companies performing translation services may charge by the word.
- Compile a style guide. You need to know the size of the paper you will be printing on in the foreign country. In the United States, 8 1/2 × 11 paper is the most common, but other countries use sizes such as A3 or A4, which would cause your writing to fill the page differently.
- Review cultural context. There are religious and ethical differences in every country to consider.
- Revise legal contracts. Be sure you understand the issues and requirements of fulfilling your contracts with foreign governments.
- International operators. If you are having trouble understanding your connection, there are operators available to assist you with translations.

- Dial an international number by adding the prefix:
  - 011 + country code + phone number
  - For example, a call from a U.S. landline in Sydney, Australia, where the country code is 61, would be 011 61 2 1234 5678.
- Electronic tools are available, such as automated currency convertors.
- Human translators are always needed to review material. They can suggest more appropriate translations.

PROJECT DEVELOPMENT

Please select one of the following cities for your translation project. After this list there is a short questionnaire to help you learn more about the city, its customs, and people.

Tokyo–Yokohama (Japan)	Ho Chi Minh City (Viet Nam)
Jakarta (Indonesia)	Bogota (Colombia)
Delhi (India)	Johannesburg-East Rand
Seoul–Incheon (South Korea)	(South Africa)
Manila (Philippines)	Taipei (Taiwan)
Karachi (Pakistan)	Onitsha (Nigeria)
Shanghai (China)	Ahmadabad (India)
Sao Paolo (Brazil)	Kuala Lumpur (Malaysia)
Mexico City (Mexico)	Caracas (Venezuela)
Moscow (Russia)	Madrid (Spain)
Shaka (Bangladesh)	Auckland (New Zealand)
Cairo (Egypt)	Casablanca (Morocco)
Bangkok (Thailand)	Guatemala City (Guatemala)
Buenos Aires (Argentina)	Damascus (Syria)
Tehran (Iran)	Jerusalem (Israel)
Istanbul (Turkey)	Riyadh (Saudi Arabia)
Lagos (Nigeria)	Doha (Qatar)
Rio de Janeiro (Brazil)	Canberra (Australia)
Kinshasa (Congo)	Montreal (Canada)
Lima (Peru)	Jakarta (Java)
Paris (France)	Frankfurt (Germany)
Lahore (Pakistan)	Prague (Czech Republic)
London (United Kingdom)	Messina (Sicily)
	Warsaw (Poland)

Investigating the Culture of Your Selection

1. The name of your city: _____
2. Main language: _____
3. International three-digit telephone code: _____
4. Currency name: _____
   Symbol for currency: _____
5. Convert $500.00 to the country's currency: _____
6. The time zone: _____
7. If it is 3:00 p.m. in your hometown, what time is it in the city you selected? _____
8. Name a favorite food in that country: _____
9. Identify a major tourist attraction in that city: _____

Project: Email Translation

You will translate the email message below to the language most often used in the city you have selected.

- Regionalize the text so there are no metaphors or phrases with double meanings.
- Use appropriate greetings and closing.
- Use articles (a, an, the) to help distinguish nouns from other parts of speech. This will reduce a lot of errors in your translation.
- Convert currency to local standards.
- Convert international phone codes for ease of dialing.
- Add a Skype address. Get one if you do not have one yet.
- Evaluate the overall quality of translation in class with other students.
- Use the format for international dates.

To whom it concerns,

My name is _____ with State University. We are writing a proposal for our engineering department for a 3D printer as ours is busted. We have $3000 in cash. We are trying to manufacture hard to find parts. Send info on your product so we can include it in our bid before ours buys the farm.

Notify us if the shipment is over 40 lbs. so we can figure in freight.

We need to have final bids down by November 10, 2020.

Give me a ring at (216) 267-1234 or my Skype address is _____

Thanks,

In the space below, rewrite the email to fix all the inappropriate words and phrases.

PEER REVIEW

There may be other students who speak the language you are using in your translation. Ask them if your translation makes sense to them. You will discover that some translation apps are better than others. Do not be offended if your translation causes some laughter, as the meaning of the translation may be completely different than what you intended.

VOCABULARY

colloquialism
digit
metaphor
regionalize

Figure Credits

Figure 17.1: Source: https://commons.wikimedia.org/wiki/File:BlankMap-World.svg.

CHAPTER EIGHTEEN

Exploring the Patent Application

Estimated time to complete: 20–30 minutes

INTRODUCTION

In this final chapter, we will analyze the patent application. It will become obvious to you that all the skills you have developed in this textbook will be helpful in fulfilling the requirements necessary to complete this document. Hopefully, this chapter will benefit you someday when you are developing your own idea for a patent either in this country or anywhere else in the world.

FIGURE 18.1 (a) USPTO Logo (b) WIPO Logo.

PROJECT OVERVIEW

Many of the skills you have developed across the various exercises in this book will enable you to assist in the writing of a patent application. As you proceed through the various steps of this patent application exercise, it will become obvious to you that the role of the technical writer is critical to the development of a patent application. The patent application is a type of proposal in that you have noticed a problem that can be solved and that you believe that your idea is the solution.

A patent is defined as: "[A] government authority or license conferring a right or title for a set period, especially the sole right to exclude others from making, using, or selling an invention."

PROJECT DESIGN

Like any other technical document, the patent has distinct headings that require very specific material. Some of the main parts of a patent[1] are:

- Specification/claims.
- The title of the invention, which should be a unique name that helps to convince the patent office of the originality of your process or invention.
- Cross-references to related applications (if any), which may be listed on an application data sheet, either instead of or together with being listed in the specification.
- A statement of federally sponsored research or development (if any).
- The names of the parties to a joint research agreement if the claimed invention was made as a result of activities within the scope of a joint research agreement.
- Reference to a sequence listing, a table, or a computer program listing appendices submitted on a

---

1 United States Patent and Trademark Office, "Patent Basics," https://www.uspto.gov/ patents-getting-started/general-information-concerning-patents, viewed March 28, 2019.

compact disc and an incorporation by reference of the material on the compact disc. The total number of compact discs, including duplicates and the files on each compact disc, shall be specified.

- Background of the invention. What led you to see the need for this item?
- Brief summary of the invention.
- Brief description with drawings (if any). Drawings can be included to demonstrate the process or item you wish to patent. It is not necessary to insert color drawings; black-and-white line drawings are acceptable. Use orthogonal or isometric drawings.
- Detailed description of the invention.
- A claim or claims section describing the capabilities of your invention.
- Abstract of the disclosure. Like every other abstract, this section is a summary of the information you wish to present to the patent office. Very often this section is written in passive voice to draw attention to the subject of the sentence. This is one of the few times passive voice is recommended.
- A nonrefundable fee is associated with every patent application. These fees start at about $200.00.

SIDE BOX 18.2:
Writing in Passive Voice

Passive voice will draw attention to the subject of the sentence, which will stress the importance of the subject of your abstract. Writers in the sciences use passive voice more often than any other writers.

PROJECT DEVELOPMENT

Performing a Patent Search

Is your idea unique, or does someone else already hold a patent on it? You should always perform a search for existing patents, often called *prior art*. Many websites are available for you to complete your search. Some are listed in Table 18.1.

TABLE 18.1 *Research existing prior art*

AGENCY/ORGANIZATION	URL	SEARCHABLE INFORMATION
U.S. Patent Office	USPTO.gov	Patent search from 1976
Espacenet	worldwide.espacenet.com	Worldwide patents
European Patent Office (EPO)	epo.org	European Union patents
Japan Patent Office (JPO)	www.jpo.go.jp/e/	Japanese patents
LexisNexis	lexisnexis.com	Prior art search
Software Patents	spi.org	Patents on apps and software

Organizing Documents

It is important to keep dated notes that are signed and witnessed by another person. As we discussed with the researcher's notebook, there should be no outside discussion of the patent information until the embargo is lifted. The embargo is lifted once the patent application is received, featured in a presentation or conference, or published in an article or book.

Do not store sensitive documents on a computer that is connected to the internet as it may be hacked from an outside source. Do not store items online where they can be detected by intruders.

Creating Persuasive Patent Drawings

The patent application requires visual elements that help to clarify complex technical drawings. Transforming informal sketches into explicit drawings is a skill. A good graphic artist must be able to recognize

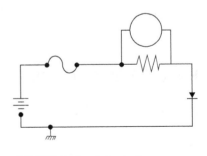

FIGURE 18.2 Rough drawing from notes.

how the object operates by viewing rough sketches of the research-er's concept.

The function of the object in Figure 18.2 is not obvious. By identifying the parts of the drawing and their functions to the graphic artist, it is possible to create a drawing that successfully depicts the process or purpose that is illustrated. The original drawing is quite different from the finished image in Figure 18.3. The image in Figure 18.3 is easier to understand, with all the sec-tions properly labeled and the details of the operation presented in a logical manner.

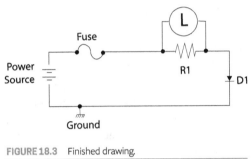

FIGURE 18.3   Finished drawing.

Provisional Application for a Patent

"Since June 8, 1995, the USPTO has offered inventors the option of filing a provisional application for patent, which was designed to provide a lower-cost first patent filing in the United States and to give U.S. applicants parity with foreign applicants. Claims and oath or declaration are NOT required for a provisional applica-tion. A provisional application provides the means to establish an early effective filing date in a patent application and permits the term 'Patent Pending' to be applied in connection with the invention. Provisional applications may not be filed for design inventions. Under United States patent law, a provisional appli-cation is a legal document filed in the United States Patent and Trademark Office (USPTO) that establishes an early filing date, but does not mature into an issued patent unless the applicant files a regular non-provisional patent application within one year."[2]

---

2   United States Patent and Trademark Office, "Patent Basics," https://www.uspto.gov/patents-getting-started/general-information-concerning-patents, viewed March 28, 2019.

Nonprovisional Application for a Patent

A nonprovisional patent application establishes the filing date for the application and starts the official USPTO examination process to determine if the invention is patentable. A nonprovisional application for a patent is made to the director of the USPTO and includes:[3]

1. A written document that comprises a specification (description and claims)
2. Drawings (when necessary)
3. An oath or declaration
4. Filing, search, and examination fees
5. A conclusion

The lessons in this text should give you the confidence to complete a patent application in a manner that is clear, well-formed, and presented in a way that the meets expectations of the person receiving it, or the user experience (UX). Technical writing can be learned by anyone.

VOCABULARY

disclosure
embargo
prior art
provision
rhetoric

Figure Credits

Figure 18.1a: Source: https://www.uspto.gov.
Figure 18.1b: Source: https://www.wipo.int.

---

3 United States Patent and Trademark Office, "Patent Basics," https://www.uspto.gov/patents-getting-started/general-information-concerning-patents, viewed March 28, 2019.